Joseph the Dreamer

A Story of Faith and Destiny

Seymour Press *SP*

Lanham, MD

Dreams of Joseph: **A Story of Faith and Destiny**

ISBN: 978-1-967034-23-9

Table of Contents

Preface

In this book, my desire is to reawaken the ancient world of Joseph, bringing its hidden patterns and overlooked moments to light. His story transcends time, offering lessons that speak with quiet power to every generation. His life unfolds as a vivid tapestry, woven with threads of faith, resilience, forgiveness, and the sovereign hand of God.

By exploring these subtle details, we are invited to recognize the treasure of God's mysterious and transformative work woven intricately into the fabric of our lives. As we reflect on Joseph's journey, the narrative draws us into a deeper appreciation for how God's hand guides, shapes, and redeems, even in circumstances that seem ordinary or forgotten.

Joseph's story speaks to the human heart as a tale of unwavering hope in the face of adversity, of divine faithfulness in seasons of uncertainty, and of redemption that heals relationships and restores what has been broken. Whether you are seeking personal encouragement, preparing a sermon, leading a small group, or simply exploring Scripture on your own, this retelling is offered to meet you where you are and invite you deeper into the unfolding story of God's grace.

As you journey through these pages, I pray that you will recognize your own reflections in Joseph's struggles and triumphs—and more importantly, that you will see the unmistakable hand of God at work, not only in his life but in yours as well. Joseph's story is far more than an ancient narrative; it is a living testimony of divine providence, a reminder that what the enemy intends for harm, God weaves into a greater good. It stands as a witness to the steadfast goodness of God.

This book has been a labor of love, shaped through prayer and reflection that I hope will draw you nearer to the heart of God, strengthen your trust in His providence, and awaken a renewed passion for Scripture. May Joseph's story remind you that God's faithfulness never wavers and His hand is always at work—quietly, powerfully, and perfectly—in the tapestry of our lives.

Chapter 1:
The Origin of Joseph's Struggle

Joseph's life finds its roots not in his own experience, but in the life of his father, Jacob. The challenges, conflicts, and perseverance that defined Jacob's journey established a pattern that Joseph would come to mirror in many ways. So, we begin with a brief story of Jacob and his struggles.

Jacob's struggles began before his birth, as he wrestled with his twin brother, Esau, in their mother's womb. This conflict disturbed their mother, Rebekah, who cried out to the Lord, "Why is this happening to me?" (Gen 25:22). In response, God revealed a profound message: "Two nations are in your womb, and two peoples from within you will be separated; one people will be stronger than the other, and the older will serve the younger" (Gen 25:23).

This wrestling match was no trivial sibling squabble. It represented a larger conflict, akin to a battle between two nations vying for supremacy. Such struggles allow no compromise; one emerges victorious, while the other succumbs and forfeits the rights to the victor. The vanquished are left to serve, assimilated into a culture that disregards the individual's identity and worth.

Jacob's struggle with Esau ended with his twin brother emerging first from the womb. By ancient standards, this gave Esau a monumental advantage. As the firstborn, he automatically inherited not only the responsibilities of headship within the family but also the privileges that came with it. This included the power to make critical decisions and a double portion of the family's inheritance.

In a society where primogeniture determined leadership, Jacob's position as second-born sealed his fate. Although his birth followed Esau's by mere moments, it relegated him to a subordinate role. His struggle in the womb had ended in apparent defeat, and the societal structures of the time left no room for reconsideration.

Yet, Jacob refused to accept his predetermined role. Driven by an insatiable desire for the privileges of the firstborn, he sought a way to change his destiny. But how could he? He could not return to his mother's womb and reverse the order of birth. Is such a rebirth possible? We know the answer to this question. A rebirth, while impossible for humans, is possible in God's kingdom. This is a recurring theme in the Bible, where the impossible becomes possible as Jesus talked about spiritual rebirth in John 3:1-21. We could be born again.

From Esau's perspective, his position as the firstborn seemed unshakable. So, he allowed himself to grow complacent and failed to value and protect his birthright. His carelessness mirrors the warning in Scripture: "Be sober-minded; be watchful. Your adversary the devil prowls around like a roaring lion, seeking someone to devour" (1 Pet 5:8).

Esau's negligence provided Jacob the opportunity he sought. In a moment of desperation, Esau sold his birthright to

Jacob for a mere bowl of red stew (Gen 25:29-33). This one-sided transaction revealed not only Jacob's cunning but also Esau's folly. How could anyone, in their right mind, so casually discard a divine privilege for such a trivial price? Esau's thoughtlessness is a cautionary tale. It is easy to condemn him, but are we not often guilty of the same attitude? We undervalue the blessings we possess and fail to appreciate their worth until they are lost.

Esau's disregard for his birthright echoes the broader story of Israel's unfaithfulness. Like Esau, the Israelites treated their divine election lightly and marginalized their covenant relationship with God. Despite being chosen as a holy nation (Deut. 7:6), they repeatedly turned away from God and pursued idols. The prophet Hosea vividly illustrates this unfaithfulness through his own life. God commanded Hosea to marry a prostitute in a symbolic act that represented Israel's spiritual adultery. For the nation had abandoned its covenant and chosen promiscuity with foreign gods over faithfulness to the Lord.

Paul's lament in Romans underscores this human propensity for failure: "As it is, it is no longer I myself who do it, but it is sin living in me. For I know that good itself does not dwell in me, that is, in my sinful nature. For I have the desire to do what is good, but I cannot carry it out" (Rom 7:18).

Like Esau and Israel, we struggle with our inability to value and protect the blessings God has delivered to us. Just as Esau relinquished his birthright for a fleeting desire, we risk losing the blessings entrusted to us when we fail to appreciate their true value. Yet, Jacob's story serves as a profound reminder that, despite human shortcomings, the redemptive power of God endures, and this power can restore destinies and transform the most dire circumstances.

Jacob's New Struggle

Over time, Jacob's struggle with his brother seemed uncomplicated, since Esau remained oblivious to Jacob's schemes and behaved recklessly. Ultimately, Jacob took advantage of Esau's foolishness. He deceived his blind father, Isaac, by pretending to be Esau and stealing the firstborn blessing. When Esau realized what had happened, he became furious and vowed to kill Jacob (Gen 27:41). But what good would revenge do? The damage was done, and the blessing, once spoken, could not be undone. The tables had turned irreversibly, and this time, he was powerless to reclaim what he had lost. Esau should have realized the importance of cherishing what he had before losing it. But he was so blinded by his own glory that he failed to see the danger and resorted to violence—the only way he knew to resolve this issue.

Although violence might seem like an immediate answer to conflict or unfairness, it ultimately is not the right solution. Violence often intensifies rather than addresses underlying issues. It often leads to retaliation and more hostility. For Jesus warned us that,"… all who draw the sword will die by the sword" (Matt 26:52). Violence not only causes physical damage, but leaves both victims and perpetrators emotionally and spiritually scarred. Though it may temporarily release frustration, it leaves long-lasting wounds that take years to heal. Sadly, Esau's desire to exact revenge became the source of Jacob's pain.

With his life in danger, Jacob fled his home under the guidance of his mother to escape his hostile brother. He journeyed to Paddan Aram, his mother's homeland, to seek refuge with his uncle, Laban. But his mother's native place was a foreign, unfamiliar land. He faced new challenges while working under Laban, a man far more crafty and deceptive than Jacob, and new struggles would define the next two decades of his life.

When Jacob fell in love for the first time, it was with Rachel, the woman he desired to marry. Laban exploited this attraction and laid a trap that tricked Jacob into marrying Leah, Rachel's older sister, first. Since Jacob still loved and desired to marry Rachel, Laban's deception forced Jacob into a polygamous marriage that became the foundation of endless family discord.

Rachel and Leah fiercely competed for Jacob's favor by having children. This competition involved their handmaids, Zilpah and Bilhah, further complicating relationships. Eventually, Jacob became father to twelve sons and one daughter born to the four women.

Jacob's struggles with Laban reached a breaking point when Laban's sons began to resent his success. They accused Jacob of "taking everything our father owned and gaining all this wealth from what belonged to our father" (Gen 31:1). Sensing the brewing hostility and growing danger of conflict, Jacob knew he could not withstand the wrath of Laban's sons and their household. At this critical moment, God intervened, commanding Jacob, "Go back to the land of your fathers and to your relatives, and I will be with you" (Gen 31:3). Trusting God's promise, Jacob took decisive action. Gathering his wives and children, loading them onto camels, and driving all his livestock and possessions ahead of him, he fled from Laban's household (Gen 31:17–18). This marked the beginning of another chapter in Jacob's life. New struggles awaited him, but so did God's continued guidance and faithfulness.

Jacob's Fear

As Jacob had successfully escaped Laban's grasp, he faced an unresolved issue. Obedient to God's command, he was returning to his father's homeland, but Esau, his old adversary, awaited him. A messenger—more like a spy—was sent ahead to Esau, and he returned with troubling news: Esau is "coming to meet you, and four hundred men are with him" (Gen 32:6).

Jacob was overwhelmed with such fear and distress, it left him paralyzed. Fear is a powerful thing. It can stop us in our tracks. He feared not only for his life but for the safety of his entire family.

In his panic, he sent them and his flocks ahead, but remained behind. There, he turned to God in prayer. "Save me, I pray, from the hand of my brother Esau, for I am afraid he will come and attack me, and also the mothers with their children" (Gen 32:11).

In this moment, Jacob struggled with a battle unlike any he had fought. He had won many struggles before, but he was helpless against this foe. All he could do was cling to God, as, in his dream-like encounter, he wrestled with a mysterious figure at the Ford of Jabbok (Gen 32:24). The wrestling match lasted not just minutes, but all night, and Jacob's perseverance did not allow him to let go. When morning came, the mysterious figure asked, "Let me go, for it is daybreak" (Gen 32:26).

Jacob released the mysterious figure because his hip was dislocated. And though he lost the physical battle, his tenacity shone through. It was Jacob's key virtue, a gift he received from God, which he valued the most. With persistence, determination, and resilience in the face of adversity, Jacob lived through many struggles. He moved toward his goals without succumbing to failures and, ultimately, achieved success despite many difficulties. This tenacity did not go unnoticed. The mysterious figure blessed him and gave him a new name, Israel, which meant that Jacob had "struggled with God and… and had overcome" (Gen 32:28).

Wrestling with God

Did Jacob wrestle with God, as the Christian tradition purports? In the context of the narrative, the identity of the mysterious figure with whom Jacob wrestled is revealed as representing the very presence of God in human form. Jacob recognized that the one with whom he was wrestling was not merely a man, but God Himself. So Jacob named the site "Peniel" (Gen 32:30), meaning "the face of God, " testifying that the figure was indeed God that he had "face to face" (Gen 32:30).

Throughout the many times that Jacob wrestled with people and challenges, his wrestling with God was the most significant. Though the Almighty God cannot be overcome by anyone or anything, in this extraordinary episode, Jacob is credited with an extraordinary feat as the "overcomer" of God. While he did not win the match, that night his perseverance and tenacity earned him this recognition.

Indeed, Jacob was blessed. Not only did he wrestle with God, but he survived the encounter. But we must not overlook that God also wrestled with Jacob, since a match requires two participants. And in His mercy, God made Himself available to Jacob as a wrestling partner.

But we should also ask, why would God engage in this struggle with Jacob? In this encounter, God's purpose was to address Jacob's fear. In reality, that is what God was wrestling with: to allow Jacob to confront fear face-to-face. In His compassion, God got His hands dirty by coming to Jacob's aid in a personal and tangible way. Although in God's divine power, God did not have to engage in this struggle, God chose to do so. Instead of remaining distant or indifferent, God met Jacob where he was and endured the same challenges and emotional strains. Jacob was not the only one sweating and struggling; God was there with him, sharing in the experience. This was remarkable; this encounter powerfully shows God's willingness to support us in our struggles and offer both strength and understanding to help us overcome fear.

The End of Jacob's Struggle with Esau

Empowered by awareness of God's presence, Jacob found the courage to move forward. Faith freed him from the paralyzing grip of fear—the faith of entrusting God, the faith of seeing God's light shining beyond the darkness, the faith that transcends our limitations and helps us see to the glory that lies beyond. Through the ordeal, he gained the trophy of faith—a symbol of triumph over his anxieties.

The chains of fear that once held Jacob captive were broken as he came to understand that while struggles would always be part of life, he could confront fear head-on. Without further hesitation, he stepped forward and went out to meet his brother

Esau. No longer hiding or lingering behind, he faced the moment with resolve.

To Jacob's surprise, Esau ran toward him, embraced him, kissed him, and they wept together (Gen 33:4). The long-standing conflict between the brothers was finally over, and they were reconciled. As the coming together of the prodigal son and his father ended the broken relationship (Lk 15:11-32), this momentous coming together marked the end of their animosity. Their relationship was restored, and there is no mention of further discord between them. After their reconciliation, Jacob settled at Kiriáth Arba (Gen 35:27).

The journey that began in turmoil ended in rest. Forced to leave his hometown at a young age, Jacob endured a solitary and challenging path in a foreign land. He might have hoped that living apart from Esau would lead to a life of peace and ease, but instead, he encountered many hardships. Yet, now in Kiriath Arba, he could finally enjoy the prosperity he had worked so hard to achieve for his family.

Yet, dark clouds loomed ominously over Jacob's head. The thunder had not yet ceased, and the tempest was not finished. Jacob's storms were far from over. In fact, they intensified as the struggle was passed down to his son, Joseph.

Chapter 2:
Joseph's Struggle

Joseph became the focal point of his family's discord, as "Israel loved Joseph more than any of his other sons, because he had been born to him in his old age" (Gen 37:3). Joseph was his father's favorite and was the only son adorned with an "ornate robe." Though the appearance of this "ornate" robe remains unclear, one thing is certain: it was not the practical garb of a shepherd. Rather, it was a luxurious garment typically reserved for a high-ranking or royal figure (e.g., Esth 8:15; Lk 15:22).

While Joseph's brothers worked diligently tending the family livestock—the family's primary source of wealth—Joseph was not assigned to this labor. Jacob had accumulated a vast number of sheep and livestock from his time with Laban and established his own estate in the Hebron Valley. All his sons were expected to care for the sheep, except for Joseph. His robe showed his father's special favor and made it clear that he did not share in the same work as his brothers. Joseph was occasionally sent on errands (e.g., Gen 37:13), but nothing that required the intense physical labor of a shepherd. His position was a privileged one, granted solely because he was Jacob's beloved favorite son.

Yet this favoritism bred resentment, as ten older brothers were competing for their father's attention and approval. We can hear their complaints: "Why does my father favor him over me?" "What does he have that I don't?" "This isn't fair." "I deserve better treatment." "How could my father do this to me?" As these thoughts simmered in the hearts of Joseph's brothers, who "saw that their father loved [Joseph] more than any of them, [and] they hated him and could not speak a kind word to him" (Gen 37:4).

So young Joseph was thrust into a hostile environment where survival seemed unlikely. His older brothers, fueled by jealousy, seethed with resentment. Yet, despite their anger, they dared not challenge their father, for in their culture, such an act would have been unthinkable. So, Joseph's brothers kept their frustration in secret— at least for the moment.

Jacob had had his mother's help to secure his birthright, but Joseph had no such advocate. His mother, Rachel, had died giving birth to Benjamin, his younger brother. This left Joseph without the maternal care and affection of a mother. Although Jacob favored him, it was not the same. He was busy managing the many responsibilities and vast wealth of a large household and couldn't offer the same care.

Joseph's only solace came from his younger brother, the only sibling who shared the same mother. However, after Rachel's death, Joseph was left to navigate his emotions alone. Beneath the outward signs of privilege of being Jacob's favorite son—wearing the special robe, and enjoying his father's affection—there lingered a quiet sadness. Joseph was torn between the glory of his status and the absence of his mother's love. What could make him happy in such a situation?

Joseph's Radical Dreams

Joseph, a dreamer, found solace in his dreams, not in the material world. One day, he had a dream unlike any other. Filled with excitement, he eagerly shared it with his brothers. He said to them: "We were binding sheaves of grain out in the field when suddenly my sheaf rose and stood upright, while your sheaves gathered around mine and bowed down to it" (Gen 37:7). He hoped they would share in the same vision and future.

Did Joseph understand the implications of his dream? His brothers immediately understood that his dream meant that Joseph would one day rule over them, as their sheaves were bowing to his. This provoked his brothers to even greater anger. Why share such a dream with his brothers, knowing it would make them resent him more? Was he arrogant?

Things took an even stranger turn when Joseph shared a similar dream. He said, in my dream, "this time the sun and moon and eleven stars were bowing down to me" (Gen 37:9). Now Joseph also told the dream to his father. But Jacob rebuked his son, for the second dream was even more significant. It implied that not only would his brothers bow to him, but also his father and mother. The dream was not complex. The sun and moon symbolized his father and mother, and the eleven stars were his brothers. Joseph was the youngest son—how could he surpass his brothers, who were years ahead of him in experience, maturity, and stature? How could he rise above them?

Recognizing the implications of the dream, Jacob's rejection was understandable. "Will your mother and I and your brothers actually come and bow down to the ground before you?" (Gen

37:10). And how could he rise above father or mother? For Jacob was the patriarch of the family and in their cultural he culture the top of the household hierarchy. The idea that a young boy could rise above his father's position was unthinkable. In their society, the father was the unquestioned head of the family, and his authority was final. How could Joseph, a mere boy, overthrow this tradition?

Despite these obstacles, Joseph believed in the possibility of God's intervention. While his family could not grasp God's power and authority, Joseph was confident that the dream God had given him would be fulfilled, even if others considered it impossible.

Joseph was not merely an arrogant brat trying to provoke his brothers. He revealed his dreams not out of arrogance, but from prophetic faith. Joseph's faith had fully embraced the dream God had given him, and the dream had taken root in his spirit. This wasn't just a figment of his imagination; it was a message from God that had to be shared, regardless of the consequences.

Like a prophet, Joseph felt compelled to speak the truth, even if it meant causing discomfort or anger, and that if he kept silent, he would have been going against God's will. He knew that God-given dreams are not mere fantasies; they would come to pass and one day become reality.

Joseph possessed spiritual discernment, a "gift" from God not given to everyone. He was committed to living in line with this privilege. Despite uncertainties about the future, he accepted the two dreams as divine revelation. Trusting God, Joseph moved forward with conviction.

Bitter Reaction to Joseph's Dreams

Jacob's reaction to his son's dreams was bitter and unfortunate. It was surprising, given his experiences with divine revelation. Had he not been a dreamer himself? Had he not seen a vision of a ladder reaching from earth to heaven? Had he not heard the voice of the Lord saying, "I am Yahweh, the God of Abraham your father and the God of Isaac. I am with you and will watch over you wherever you go, and I will bring you back to this land. I will not leave you until I have done what I have promised you." (Gen 28:13, 15) Did not God reveal Himself and His plans through dreams?

Many years had passed since Jacob's own divine encounter, and he may have thought such revelations were reserved for a chosen few like himself, not for a young, untested boy like Joseph. Nevertheless, Jacob's reaction was not justifiable.

Our ego often prevents us from accepting what seems unlikely. Jacob struggled with the idea that, one day, he might bow down to his young and immature son. A son he could not yet see as a leader. His eyes were on the helpless young boy before him, and he could not see beyond present appearances. Our ego can make it hard to accept the significance of a humble boy. "How could I bow down to you?" The thought of it felt intolerable. Surely, this was the way that Pharisees must have felt when they saw Jesus. How could I bow down to this humble figure and call him my Savior, the Messiah?"

We often fail to see beyond our immediate circumstances. We overlook the bigger picture, feeling most concerned with our immediate pressing challenges, knowledge, or problems. Future steps feel distant, so we focus on the current demands of our lives. For this reason, we judge others and ourselves by present appearances, sometimes falling into self-pity.

However, we aren't at fault. Our social structure drives this pattern. We rush from one task to task, communicate constantly with everyone on our contact list, handle hundreds of problems, and put out the fires, and rarely take time to consider the bigger picture. With the constant information at our fingertips, we are swept up in the rapid-paced digital present. Where is our future, our big picture, our goal?

We must take time to dream—to transcend our current situations and see beyond them. Dreams offer us a vision that is not confined to a time or place; they enable us to perceive something greater than what we know now. As psychiatrist and philosopher Carl Jung once said, dreams can be a gateway to metaphysical realms, even to the divine. Without them, we risk remaining trapped in the immediate, physical world.

Faith and dreams are closely linked. Faith allows us to transcend physical limits through dreaming. When accompanied by faith, dreams offer insight into divine greatness, elevate us to the realms of God, allowing us to glimpse into His grandeur and mystery.

Inside Matters

Jacob's doubt about God's choice of Joseph is understandable. Why did God reveal such a significant plan to Joseph and not to the others? Wasn't Jacob the most qualified to receive such a revelation? Though Eve Jacob had grown somewhat distant from God because of his busy life, why couldn't God have chosen one of his ten older sons—each of them more mature and wise than Joseph?

As was clearly evident in Samuel's search for Israel's future king, God values what is inside a person more than what is on the outside. God told Samuel, "Yahweh does not look at the things people look at. People look at the outward appearance, but Yahweh looks at the heart" (1 Sam 16:7).

When Samuel was tasked with anointing the next king, he was sent to Jesse's house. But when Jesse presented his eldest son first, then each of the others, God rejected them all.

Puzzled at this turn of events, Samuel asked, "Are these all your sons?" Jesse then mentioned his youngest son, David, who was tending the sheep, and this least likely candidate was the one God chose. Because God saw what others could not. He chose a mere shepherd boy, because David was a man after God's own heart (1 Sam 13:14)—a man who put God first and had an intimate, personal relationship with Him. The relationship he had with God wasn't superficial; it was a heart-to-heart connection.

Joseph, like David, had a heart-to-heart relationship that was pure enough to see God's plan. He could dream the impossible because he was aligned with God's heart. Further, his youth and innocence protected him from the corruption that might have come with age. Joseph, however, was too young to participate in such atrocities—Benjamin had not yet been born. Joseph was the only one pure, without any blood on his hands.

Joseph, like David, maintained a close and pure relationship with God, which enabled him to understand God's plan and dream big. His youth and innocence kept him from the corruption his older brothers experienced; he did not partake in their violent acts, leaving him as the only one without blood on his hands.

Had he been older, he might have joined his brothers in the violent actions they took, such as those of Simeon and Levi, who massacred the Hivites to avenge Dinah's defilement (Gen 34:5-29). His brothers, fueled by anger, took their swords, slaughtered the men of the city, and plundered the goods. Jacob, horrified by their actions, fled with his family to Bethel to escape the consequences of their atrocity. But Joseph remained untouched by such violence. He maintained his purity, unaffected by the corruption around him.

Joseph was pure in heart, just as David was, which is why he was chosen for a divine purpose. His uncorrupted heart made him suitable to receive God's revelation—a dream with a significant role in salvation, not only for his family but for the world. This divine plan was revealed through a dream so unlikely, so unimaginable that no one could fully understand its significance at the time, and only someone as pure and blameless as Joseph could fulfill this plan.

Chapter 3:
Faith Pilgrimage in the Unknown

Faith is a pilgrimage. Faith is not merely a struggle we experience but a profound journey we endure. It propels us into the unknown and demands strength, perseverance, and trust in the face of overwhelming odds. For Joseph, it was time to take his pilgrimage of faith, a journey he was destined to embark on whether he felt prepared or not. Faith isn't just something we wrestle with; it's a deep and lasting journey that we experience.

Jacob assigned Joseph a seemingly easy task—a harmless errand. He told him, "Your brothers are grazing the flocks near Shechem… I am going to send you to them," Go and see if all is well with your brothers and with the flocks, and bring word back to me" (Gen 37:13-14). Without hesitation, Joseph set out to fulfill his father's instructions.

Yet, Jacob's decision was perplexing. Did he not realize the danger his older sons posed? They hied out a brutal massacre, slaughtering all the males of a city to avenge their sister. Jacob must have known how violent they could be and how jealous they were of Joseph and how strongly they resented him because of their father's favoritism and his dreams. Why would Jacob send him into such a precarious situation?

Perhaps he underestimated the depth of his sons' bitterness. For surely they would not harm their own flesh and blood. Jacob often avoided confronting his sons' misdeeds. His unwillingness to discipline them may have blinded him to the state of their hearts. Had Jacob, like his brother Esau, demonstrated complacent ignorance, not recognizing the gravity of the situation?

But Jacob was not alone in his ignorance; Joseph demonstrated naivety. He must have known his brothers harbored animosity toward him. His awareness of family dynamics would have alerted him to the risks. Yet, he obeyed his father without hesitation. His willingness to undertake this dangerous mission reveals a pure and trusting heart that valued obedience over self-preservation.

Joseph's decision to go despite the danger marked the beginning of his faith pilgrimage. This simple errand was a defining moment—a threshold into a journey filled with trials, betrayals, and revelations. This journey would not only refine Joseph's character but also reveal God's greater purpose.

As seen in Joseph's obedience, faith is not about having all the answers or knowing what lies ahead. It is about stepping into uncertainty while trusting God's plan. Joseph's willingness to embrace the unknown, despite the risks, reflects the essence of true faith. This pilgrimage challenges us to trust God's wisdom and see every step, no matter how perilous, as part of a divine design. For this errand to Shechem was far more than a father's request—it was the first step into a path that would lead him into the heart of God's redemptive plan for his family and for nations beyond.

Facing the Fate

Joseph's innocence showed his sincere, uncalculated nature. He accepted his fate directly, without looking for an escape route, much like others who demonstrated deep faith. For example, Jesus knowingly accepted death to complete His mission, and Abraham obeyed God's command to offer his beloved son Isaac as a sacrifice, travelling for three days to Mount Moriah with this knowledge.

The essence of faith is unwavering obedience in the face of uncertainty. Genuine faith accepts God's word and will as absolute and acts upon it with steadfast conviction that God's way is the only way.

But is this a blind faith? No, it is far from blind. Blind faith places trust in something or someone without a foundation, reason, or evidence. Faith in God is built on a solid foundation of God's own character and works. We trust God because God is trustworthy. He saves, He cares, and He makes a way where there is none. Joseph's journey revealed this truth. Despite his dire circumstances, God consistently provided a way forward. Though Joseph could not see the full picture, his faith allowed him to trust in God's guidance.

Such bold, trusting, and resolute faith requires surrender of the human tendency to control and calculate. It invites us to lean entirely on God's promises, knowing that His plans are higher than ours and that His ways will ultimately lead to life and salvation. Joseph's story is a testament to this truth, showing how faith is a journey of alignment with God's divine purposes.

Lost and Found

Joseph's pilgrimage began with his wandering. The Bible tells us, "He was wandering around in the fields." (Gen 37:15) This seemingly simple yet significant detail reflects a common aspect of spiritual journeys—starting from a place of being lost. It mirrors the Israelites' forty years of wandering in the wilderness, a time when they, too, were learning to trust God's guidance. Pilgrimages often begin this way, as we find ourselves disoriented, unsure of the path ahead, and searching for direction.

Joseph's inexperience played a role in his wandering. Having seldom ventured far from home, he was unfamiliar with the land. When the seemingly identical fields stretched endlessly in every direction, he quickly lost his bearings. This was a metaphor for the early stages of a faith journey. When the road is unfamiliar and the horizon unclear, we face moments of being spiritually lost.

However, pilgrimage is not just about wandering; it is also about exploration. Though dangers surround us, it is essential to take the next step into the unknown. Faith requires courage to face trials and challenges. When our strength fails, we depend on God's power as Zechariah reminds us, "Not by might nor by power, but by my Spirit," says the Lord Almighty (Zech 4:6). Our steps forward are fueled by what God can accomplish through us, even when we feel inadequate or unsure.

Joseph did not wander for long. A man found him and pointed him in the right direction: "They have moved on from here; I heard them say, 'Let's go to Dothan'" (Gen 37:17). As this encounter reminds us, God often provides guidance through unexpected means. This seemingly incidental encounter with an unnamed "man" became a vital part of Joseph's journey. Without his help, Joseph might have returned home without ever finding his brothers stepping into the divine plan awaiting him.

Dothan lay about twelve miles from Shechem, a distance that would take several hours to traverse. The journey was no small task. What was intended to be a brief errand became an arduous excursion because Joseph's brothers had moved. But this detour also held significance. Why were his brothers in Shechem?

Shechem was the site where Simeon and Levi had slaughtered the city's men in vengeance for Dinah's defilement (Gen 34:25-29). It was a place of infamy for Jacob's family, marked by violence and bitter memories that Jacob likely wished to avoid. Yet, his sons returned there, perhaps out of defiance or a lingering connection to the land. Knowing his sons' volatile nature, Jacob not only sent Joseph to check on the flocks, but also to prevent further conflict with the remaining inhabitants or neighboring tribes.

Joseph's task was more than delivering a simple report. It was a mission to safeguard the family's stability, a responsibility thrust upon a young man already despised by his brothers. Despite the dangers, Joseph pressed on, and diligence and determination eventually brought him to Dothan, where he found his brothers—and unknowingly stepped into the next phase of God's unfolding plan for his life.

Hungry for Power

Joseph's brothers saw him from a distance; his distinctive, ornate robe immediately gave him away. In their isolated, barren surroundings, who else could it be but Joseph, the boy who flaunted his favored status? Their bitterness boiled over as one shouted, "Here comes that dreamer!" Their resentment was deeply rooted — not merely in the robe, but in the dreams Joseph had shared, dreams that foretold his rise above them. The thought that their youngest brother might one day rule over them was unbearable.

At first glance, it's easy to vilify Joseph's brothers, but their actions expose something universal: the human hunger for power. We are all guilty of this to some degree. Deep down, we all yearn to climb to the top, to assert dominance, and to avoid the indignity of being trampled. No one relishes the thought of living as a doormat, constantly at the mercy of others. Power offers security, influence, and the ability to shape our own destiny.

This drive for power is hardwired into our nature. Evolutionists argue it's a survival instinct, a mechanism for ensuring that the fittest thrive in a world governed by competition. While this perspective holds some truth, it's not the full picture. We are not merely creatures of survival; our yearning for power often transcends survival, veering into pride, ambition, and a desire for control.

Joseph's brothers were acting on this innate drive. They considered him a threat that needed to be eliminated and conspired to kill him. To them, he was like a cancer threatening the family's unity and hierarchy. But Joseph was just a boy, helpless against his older, stronger brothers. The true threat wasn't Joseph—it was the fear he represented.

Their fear stemmed from unmet needs and unfulfilled desires in a family marked by rivalry, as the brothers competed for their father's approval and jostled for position in the pecking order. Their struggle mirrors the human quest for recognition. The same question has driven empires, wars, and personal ambitions: Who is the greatest?

Jesus' disciples wrestled with this question. They argued among themselves about who was the greatest in the kingdom of God. Perceiving their thoughts, Jesus disrupted their worldly view of power with a profound truth: "If anyone would be first, he must be last of all and servant of all" (Mk 9:33-37).

His statement challenges worldly values. In God's kingdom, greatness is not measured by dominance but by humility, service, and self-sacrifice. Jesus radically reversed the worldly hierarchy. The "last" in this world—those who humble themselves, serve others, and put others' needs above their own—are the "first" in His kingdom. For the value systems of this world and God's kingdom are fundamentally different. What is esteemed as "first" in human eyes—power, status, wealth— matters little in God's economy.

This challenges our natural hunger for power and invites us to redefine greatness as service and humility. Joseph's brothers, blinded by their desire for power and recognition, failed to see that fulfillment lies in unity, love, and faith—not domination.

Brother's Fear and Anger

Fear and anger are cousins—inseparable companions that feed off each other. They thrive in insecurity. When we feel insecure, we are overwhelmed by both fear and anger. These emotions also bring jealousy, hopelessness, and low self-esteem. Insecurity clouds judgment, blinds us to reason, and leaves us vulnerable to destructive impulses. This was the reality for Joseph's brothers.

Overcome by insecurity, they saw no alternative but to destroy the source of their torment—Joseph. Their decision to kill him wasn't strange; they had taken lives before. They slaughtered all the men in the entire city of Shechem. Since the brutality of their actions left them hardened and caused moral decay, it was easy for their calloused hearts to contemplate greater evil.

Their fear and anger toward Joseph weren't simply about his dreams or their father's preferential treatment of him. They were symptoms of deeper, unmet needs—for affirmation, love, and a sense of belonging. But instead of addressing their grievances, they allowed bitterness to fester, making Joseph a scapegoat for their pain.

The Bible reminds us that this pattern is not unique to Joseph's brothers. Throughout Scripture, we see similar acts of violence rooted in fear and anger. Cain killed Abel because his offering was rejected, while Abel's was accepted (Gen 4:3-8). Absalom killed Amnon in a quest for vengeance (2 Sam. 13:28-29). One of the most horrifying examples occurs in Judges 19-21, when the tribes of Israel banded together to attempt to annihilate the tribe of Benjamin in a brutal civil war. These acts reveal how unchecked fear, anger, and insecurity can spiral into violence and devastation.

Joseph's ordeal was no different. His brothers' anger and fear of losing power and standing set the stage for betrayal. For Joseph, the "day of horror" had begun. He was surrounded by hatred and had no way to escape his brothers' wicked intentions.

In the midst of their dark conspiracy, help came unexpectedly. Reuben, the eldest brother, intervened. "'Let's not take his life. 'Don't shed any blood. Throw him into this cistern in the wilderness, but don't lay a hand on him.' Reuben said this to rescue him and take him back to his father." (Gen 37:21-22) These words provided hope amidst the darkness. While his motivation is unclear—was he protecting Joseph, or attempting to restore his own standing with their father? Yet not all the brothers were wholly consumed by hatred. Reuben demonstrated that even in a world of fear and anger, compassion and reason can break through.

Broken Empathy

In the past, Reuben had committed a grievous mistake against his father that fractured their relationship, and he seemed determined to avoid repeating his error. While Reuben likely shared the resentment his brothers harbored toward Joseph, he understood how deeply his father loved Joseph. And his love and concern for his father outweighed his personal feelings. His empathy—however flawed—allowed him to take a step back and see the situation differently.

Such empathy can transform our perspective. When we "feel" for others, we begin to "see" the world through their eyes.

Bernard Meland's concept of "appreciative consciousness" encapsulates this idea: empathy is not just about understanding but about interpreting our own circumstances in light of others' experiences and emotions. It enables a deeper, relational knowledge that bridges gaps between individuals.

This I-Thou relationship, as Martin Buber described it, has the potential to halt cycles of violence and destruction. Many horrors recounted in Scripture—Cain's murder of Abel, the betrayal of Joseph's brothers, the war against the Benjamites—are rooted in a failure of empathy. When we fail to feel for others, we lose sight of the consequences of our actions. However, cultivating empathy is challenging because our lives are dominated by selfishness at the genetic level. Ego becomes our master, and we, its slaves.

For a brief moment, Reuben's appeal broke through the hardened hearts of his brothers. They listened to him and refrained from killing Joseph. Instead, they stripped him of his ornate robe—a symbol of their envy and bitterness—and threw him into an empty cistern. The place was deep, dark, and devoid of life, like the emotional chasm that had developed between Joseph and his brothers.

But their fleeting compliance with Reuben's plea soon gave way to another wicked scheme. As Midianite merchants passed by, the brothers decided to sell Joseph for twenty shekels of silver (Gen 37:28). They rationalized that this was better than killing him. They had spared his life and profited from the transaction.

While they believed they had found a "win-win" solution, their satisfaction was short-lived. They were blind to the true horror of their actions. Selling Joseph into slavery was not an act of mercy; it was a betrayal of the deepest kind. In some ways, it was worse than killing him, for they condemned their brother to a life of unimaginable suffering.

Slavery, in any form, is a stain on humanity. Harriet Ann Jacobs, a former slave and abolitionist, captured its horrors in her writing: "There are wrongs which even the grave does not bury." Slavery strips individuals of their dignity, subjecting them to inhumane treatment that defies comprehension. It grants unchecked power to the oppressor, which turns man into a beast driven by cruelty and domination.

Joseph's brothers, consumed by jealousy and blinded by their selfish desires, became agents of this human horror. They reduced their own flesh and blood to a commodity to be traded for profit. What they failed to grasp was the depth of the wound they inflicted—not only on Joseph but also to themselves. In their attempt to rid themselves of a perceived rival, they enslaved their hearts to guilt, regret, and brokenness.

Injustice

The brothers sold Joseph into slavery without a second thought about his future. They did not care how a young boy could survive in such a cruel world. They had effectively condemned him to a slow, lingering death. The prospect of survival as a slave seemed worse than death itself, leaving Joseph with no hope but perhaps to pray for a swift end to his misery.

This heinous act occurred while Reuben was away. When he returned and discovered what his brothers had done, he was deeply grieved by their actions and tore his clothes—a traditional sign of mourning and distress.

Reuben's pain wasn't merely for Joseph; it was also for his father, Jacob. How could he face him without Joseph? How could he explain this unthinkable betrayal? Reuben knew this was not just another misstep but a sin so grave it could shatter the fragile bond between Jacob and his sons. Jacob might never forgive them. This would tip the scales of his father's patience and love.

Seeing Reuben's agony, the other brothers began to realize the weight of their actions. What they had done was not the pragmatic solution they had convinced themselves it was—it was a devastating betrayal. But the deed was done, and there was no turning back. Now, they had to return to their father without Joseph, knowing their guilt would invite his wrath. Desperate to avoid Jacob's fury, they devised a deceitful plan to cover their tracks.

They took Joseph's ornate robe, the symbol of their envy, slaughtered a goat, and dipped the robe in its blood to fabricate a story. This false narrative painted Joseph's demise as the work of a wild animal. The innocent goat became a stand-in for Joseph, its blood serving as a grim testament to their lies and an attempt to conceal their guilt. Surely, only the blood can cover up their shame.

When Jacob saw the bloodied robe, he cried out in anguish, "It is my son's robe! Some ferocious animal has devoured him. Joseph has surely been torn to pieces" (Gen 37:33). Jacob's assumption, though false, became his reality. Overwhelmed with grief, he accepted this narrative without questioning its truth. None of the brothers dared to speak up. Silence sealed their deception.

The plan seemed to work. Their guilt was momentarily buried under the guise of sacrifice. With the innocent goat's blood, their sins were covered, and they were spared the wrath of their father. But this false freedom came at the cost of Jacob's heartbreak and Joseph's suffering.

Meanwhile, Joseph's fate was sealed. He was sold to Potiphar, a high-ranking official in Pharaoh's court in Egypt. Far from home, Joseph found himself in a foreign land with no allies, no family, and seemingly no hope. What could he do to escape this nightmare? Who could possibly help him in such dire circumstances?

The psalmist once asked a similar question: "I lift up my eyes to the mountains—where does my help come from?" (Ps 121:1). The answer followed swiftly: "My help comes from Yahweh, the Maker of heaven and earth" (Ps 121:2). For Joseph, the same Yahweh was still present, who watched over him in the depths of his suffering. For though Joseph could not yet see it, God's hand was at work. Yahweh, the one who made heaven and earth, was more than capable of delivering him. The faithful recognize that even in the darkest moments, God's providence remains steadfast and offers hope and redemption.

Chapter 4:
God's Success and Favor

From the preceding narrative, we might naturally assume that Joseph's life will be full of misery and despair. The life of a slave offers no promise of glory. It is intrinsically tied to pain and relentless toil—realities woven into the very fabric of slavery. These hardships are rarely discussed; oppressors conceal their actions, while the oppressed endure in silence under the crushing load of their plight.

Joseph seemed destined for this same fate as countless slaves throughout history. His own brothers betrayed cast him into the darkest and most desolate depths of the abyss of life. And he had hit rock bottom. Yet his story takes an unexpected turn. Remarkably, Joseph did not just survive—he was successful and thrived.

How could this be? The answer lies in a single truth: "The Lord was with Joseph so that he prospered" (Genesis 39:2). God's presence was the defining factor in Joseph's success. It was not a result of his own ability, resources, or effort. As a young slave boy with no power to change his situation, Joseph's success was entirely a manifestation of God's grace.

Two Hebrew words in Genesis 39 highlight Joseph's success. The first word is *masliah,* meaning "to be successful" or "to prosper," which appears 65 times in the Old Testament, with three occurrences in Genesis 39, all describing Joseph's success. However, this is not ordinary success —it is deeply spiritual. Consider how Abraham's servant, was sent to Paddan Aram to find a wife for Isaac. Faced with the seemingly impossible task of locating the right woman in an unfamiliar land, the servant prayed earnestly for God's intervention. He sought the success—*masliah*—that could only come from divine guidance (Gen 24:12).

The young slave's prosperity did not result from human effort. God orchestrated the events of his life. Thus, *masliah* underscores the reality that while human efforts and diligence matter, true success is a gift from God. For Joseph, every remarkable achievement testified to God's providence, not just to his personal capability.

The second word, *hen*, often translated as "favor" or "grace," is inherently theological. Genesis 39:3-4 explains, "When his master saw that the Lord was with him and that the Lord gave him success in everything he did, Joseph found favor [*hen*] in his eyes." Because Potiphar recognized Joseph's unique success, he entrusted him with his entire household. Such elevation and credibility did not result from natural charisma or skill. I was because divine favor—*hen*—resting upon him.

God's unmerited grace, gracious presence, and provision in Joseph's life softened Potiphar's heart so that Joseph rose from a lowly slave to the overseer of an influential household.

The interplay between *masliah* (success) and *hen* (favor) demonstrates that success rooted in God's grace transcends human limitations. It defies circumstances, redefines expectations, and glorifies the divine. Joseph's journey teaches us that even in the lowest and darkest moments, trusting and depending on God can turn the situation in our favor.

Faith Shines in Darkness

Faith shines its brightest when we are walking through the valley of the shadow of death. It serves as the bedrock of our strength because it anchors us in God, who promises to be with us in every circumstance. As David proclaimed, "I will fear no evil, for you are with me" (Psalm 23:4). Faith allows us to perceive the unseen presence and power of God actively working behind the scenes. It allows us to recognize that God's hand is lifting us up when nothing in our circumstances seems to propel us forward. With this assurance, no situation is too bleak or overwhelming for us to overcome.

Despite being sold into slavery and enduring great hardship, Joseph's life became a conduit of blessing for "the Lord blessed the household of the Egyptian because of Joseph" (Gen 39:5). For God's blessings extend to those who do not acknowledge Him, as long as there is a mediating source. Thus, Joseph's faith and God's presence in his life became the channel through which blessings flowed to all those in his proximity.

Had Joseph's brothers understood this principle, they might have thought twice before selling him into slavery. Yet their act of betrayal was used by God to sovereignly position Joseph as a source of blessing, demonstrating that faith, paired with God's favor, can redeem the darkest situations.

We often seek tangible ways to invite fortune and blessings. People often rely on superstitions, whether it's carrying lucky items like a rabbit's foot or performing rituals with special objects, hoping these actions will bring good fortune. These tokens bring a sense of comfort, as many believe they are conduits for divine favor. However, the prophet Isaiah starkly critiques the futility of such practices as fashioning wood as a god and worshipping it" (Is 44:15).

He points out the folly of idolatry in that people take materials created by God—wood, metal, or stone—and fashion them into objects of worship, attributing to them powers they do not possess. This misplaced trust blinds their understanding. Further, he observes, "Their eyes are plastered over so they cannot see, and their minds closed so they cannot understand" (Isaiah 44:18). What we need is the eye of faith, not reliance on material objects or empty rituals. Such faith in God opens our eyes to the active presence and guidance of the true source of all blessings.

Post-Easter Christians understand that our faith must rest in Jesus Christ, the resurrected Lord. He is not only the source of every blessing but also the ultimate mediator through whom those blessings flow. As Paul writes, "For there is one God and one mediator between God and mankind, the man Christ Jesus" (1 Tim 2:5). Unlike charms or superstitions, faith in Christ addresses the root of human fears and offers real solutions to life's challenges. Christ's redemptive work assures us that He is with us, empowering us to bring God's blessings to our communities. Like Joseph, we can become channels of divine favor, reflecting God's grace to those around us.

Surely, faith in God can dismantle the superstitions that haunt us. No charm, idol, or ritual can replace the transformative power of trusting in the living God. These empty practices may temporarily soothe fears, but they cannot solve life's real problems or bring lasting peace. Instead, when we place our faith in Christ—the one who was, who is, and who is to come—we align ourselves with the source of all blessings. Through Him, we can shine light into the darkness, becoming vessels of His grace and favor in a broken world.

Joseph's First Temptation

Life is a journey filled with unpredictable highs and lows. Even those who walk in God's favor are not exempt from trials and temptations. Though blessed with God's success and favor, Joseph was no exception to this reality. His life of betrayal and hardship exemplified resilience and faith. Yet, his greatest test came from an unexpected source—Potiphar's wife.

Noticing Joseph's striking appearance, that he was "well-built and handsome," Potiphar's wife brazenly attempted to seduce him, urging him to "come to bed with me" (Gen 39:6-7).

This might have been a strong temptation for young Joseph, appealing to his physical desires and the lure of power. If he had accepted, he could have gained dominion over Potiphar's entire household, including his wife. For a slave who rose from humble beginnings, the opportunity for this level of control could have been intoxicating. Yet, Joseph's response reveals a character deeply committed to integrity and faith.'

This episode mirrors the devil's temptation of Jesus in the wilderness. Satan presented Jesus with the splendor of the world's kingdoms and promised them to him in exchange for his worship. The allure of power and glory was immense, but Jesus stood firm and rebuked him, "Away from me, Satan! For it is written: 'Worship the Lord your God, and serve Him only'" (Matt 4:10).

Like Jesus, Joseph rejected temptation and refused to compromise his principles for fleeting gratification. When confronted by Potiphar's wife, he articulated with striking clarity: "My master has withheld nothing from me except you, because you are his wife. How then could I do such a wicked thing and sin against God?" (Gen 39:9).

Joseph's refusal rested on two pillars that were unshakable for him: loyalty to Potiphar and faithfulness to God. Joseph recognized the profound trust his master had placed in him. To betray that trust by taking his wife would not only be an act of injustice but a personal affront to a man who had elevated him to a position of authority. Loyalty demanded that he honor this trust in the face of temptation.

More importantly, Joseph's refusal was rooted in his faith. He understood that sin is not merely an ethical lapse but a direct offense against God. Joseph's success and favor came from God, and to succumb to temptation would be to spurn the One who had faithfully guided him. This unwavering commitment enabled him to resist a seemingly irresistible offer.

Temptation often presents itself as an opportunity for gain or fulfillment, cloaked in the guise of immediate satisfaction. Yet, as Joseph demonstrates, no promise of fleeting pleasure or power is worth compromising one's integrity or relationship with God. His ability to withstand such pressure underscores the importance of grounding our actions in faith and moral conviction.

Moreover, Joseph's narrative reveals that true strength doesn't come from willpower alone, but from reliance on God, who equips us to stand firm through seemingly insurmountable challenges. Joseph's commitment to righteousness, at great personal cost, reflects the transformative power of faith.

Temptation is a universal challenge that preys on our vulnerabilities and desires. Yet, the stories of Joseph and Jesus remind us that we can overcome by trusting in God's strength and prioritizing His will above all else. Their examples inspire us to remain faithful, even when doing so is difficult.

More Troubles

The enemy is unyielding in its pursuit of our downfall, deaf to reason and relentless in its attack. His ultimate goal is our destruction. This truth becomes evident in the narrative of Joseph's encounter with Potiphar's wife. Her desperation escalated to the point where she physically grabbed him, demanding once again, "Come to bed with me" (Gen 39:12). At that moment, Joseph had no room for negotiation or debate. He chose the only honorable and effective course of action—he left his cloak in her hand and ran out of the house" (Gen 39:12). Running away is not always a sign of weakness, but the wisest response to an unavoidable temptation or attack.

Joseph's decision to flee was an act of integrity, but it came at a great cost. Potiphar's wife concocted a narrative to protect her pride and manipulate the situation. She told her husband that Joseph had "mocked," ridiculed, or humiliated her. She alleged that Joseph entered her bedroom to "mock" and shame her by undressing in her presence. In her version, she screamed for help, and Joseph fled, leaving behind the damning evidence of his cloak.

This accusation flipped Joseph's reputation for fidelity and uprightness on its head. His commitment to living an honest, trustworthy life seemed to have worked against him. On hearing his wife's plea for justice, Potiphar "burned with anger" (Gen 39:19). His unfounded response was swift. The circumstantial evidence—the discarded cloak and his wife's testimony carried the weight of a trusted source. For him, there was no need for further inquiry, for the case against Joseph was straightforward and damning.

Joseph's story highlights that, sometimes, doing the right thing does not lead to immediate reward or vindication. Instead, it may result in misunderstanding, false accusations, and unjust consequences. Despite Joseph's innocence and refusal to compromise, he was condemned.

This narrative reveals that the enemy often uses circumstances and people to turn integrity into vulnerability and righteousness into grounds for attack. However, Joseph's response to temptation and the subsequent injustice demonstrates a critical lesson for believers. His actions reflect unwavering faith and trust in God's ultimate justice, when the immediate outcome seems dire.

Our commitment to integrity may not always shield us from hardship. However, it positions us within the will of God, where His sovereignty reigns supreme. Joseph's willingness to endure the consequences of his flight from temptation exemplifies a life surrendered to God's purposes, aware that God's plan would ultimately prevail.

The enemy's relentless schemes are not the final answer. While Joseph's situation appeared bleak, his story was far from over. God would use this unjust episode to further His plan for Joseph's life and the salvation of many. This truth encourages us to remain steadfast in the face of trials, knowing that God can transform the most unjust circumstances into avenues for His glory. Joseph's choice to face unjust consequences was not the end of his journey but a pivotal moment eventual redemption. For those who face similar trials, his example serves as a beacon of hope. So, we should never give up on God, even in the face of relentless attacks.

God With Us

The dark chapter of Joseph's imprisonment demonstrated God's unwavering presence. Despite having the authority to execute Joseph for the alleged crime, Potiphar chose to imprison him. His act of restraint might have stemmed from Joseph's earlier favor in Potiphar's household or perhaps lingering doubts about his wife's accusations. Whatever the reason, sparing Joseph's life was a testament to God's providence, ensuring the continuation of God's plan for Joseph.

Even so, Joseph's situation was dire. He was in prison for a crime he did not commit—a circumstance that could easily provoke despair and doubt. This was an opportune moment for Joseph to echo the lament of the psalmist: "My God, my God, why have you forsaken me? Why are you so far from saving me, so far from my cries of anguish?" (Ps 22:1). These words encapsulate the universal cry of humanity in times of suffering and silence. When God's intervention seems delayed or absent, we question God's presence and wonder if God has forgotten us.

Yet, God is neither absent nor inactive. God's work often unfolds behind the scenes, invisible but impactful. For Joseph, God's presence became evident within the confines of prison.

"While there, Yahweh was with him; he showed him kindness (*hased*) and granted him favor (*hen*) in the eyes of the prison warden" (Gen 39:21). Here, the theological formula of God's blessing resurfaces because God was with Joseph, he experienced kindness and favor. These gifts did not stem from human effort but directly from God's character.

The Hebrew term *hased* is rich in meaning, encompassing mercy, lovingkindness, and steadfast love. It reflects God's covenantal loyalty and unwavering commitment to His people. In Joseph's life, this kindness became tangible through the favor he found with the prison warden. Despite his unjust circumstances, Joseph's relationship with God transformed his environment. His faith and integrity allowed him to remain a channel for divine blessing in a most unlikely place.

For "The Lord was with Joseph and gave him success in whatever he did" (Gen 39:23). Again, the term *masliah* signifies not just prosperity but divine enablement—success granted by God's power. Joseph's unique relationship with God ensured that he thrived wherever he was placed, whether in Potiphar's house or a prison cell. His faithfulness became a reflection of God's faithfulness, for that success is not dependent on external circumstances but on God's presence.

In our own seasons of hardship, Joseph's story encourages us to trust in God's presence and providence. When we walk through dark valleys, we can be assured that God is with us, granting us strength and favor. Just as Joseph's faithfulness made him a vessel of blessing, we can be the conduit of blessings to everyone, no matter where we find ourselves.

Life in Prison

Despite Joseph earning favor from the prison warden, he endured years of discomfort and isolation. Living in prison has never been easy, but ancient prisons were especially harsh. Unlike modern facilities, which often provide basic amenities like beds and toilets, ancient prisons were unrelentingly grim. They were filthy, cramped, and devoid of any comfort—a far cry from the most rudimentary standards of today. Some contemporary European prisons might resemble a college dormitory, but Joseph's reality was closer to a dungeon: dark, unclean, and suffocatingly oppressive. Though he was trusted with responsibility, Joseph remained trapped in the "pit" of despair. Yet, Joseph held onto something vital: his dreams.

In the darkest of circumstances, dreams provide a glimmer of hope and a way forward. We cannot survive by merely enduring harsh realities; We must regularly dream to see beyond their immediate condition.

Poet and playwright, Oscar Wilde described a dreamer as, "one who can only find his way by moonlight, and his punishment is that he sees the dawn before the rest of the world." This poetic insight captures the paradox of dreaming: it is both a blessing and a burden. Dreamers see the faintest glimmers of hope and possibility even in the midst of darkness. For Joseph, dreams became his moonlight, guiding him toward God's purposes despite the confines of the prison.

The story of Jacob's ladder highlights the power of a dream that connects the earthly to the divine. In his dream, Jacob saw a ladder reaching from earth to heaven, with angels ascending and descending it. This vision was not merely a fantastical image; it symbolized the interconnectedness of God's realm and the human experience. The ladder was a medium of transcendence, a bridge that closed the gap between our finite struggles and the infinite presence of God. Jacob's ladder represents the reality that even when we are confined by the limitations of this world, there is a divine connection to something greater. Using the ladder, Jacob was able to move beyond his immediate fears and encounter the vastness of God's promise.

Like him, Joseph experienced transcendence through dreams. From a young age, he understood these visions as God's divine guidance, treating them seriously and seeking their meaning with faith. His attentiveness to these dreams allowed him to see opportunities where others saw only despair. He treated every faint "moonlight" of God's revelation seriously, even when it seemed too dim for others to notice. While his surroundings were bleak, his attuned to God's purposes gave him the strength to endure hardship and rise above his circumstances.

Dreams connect us with God's greater narrative for our lives. In them, we step outside the constraints of our immediate reality and see divine possibilities. For Joseph, dreams were his ladder to the divine and his hope in hopeless situations. They sustained him through years of waiting and prepared him for the day when they would become reality. For even in the darkest pits, we can find light by dreaming beyond reality, trusting that God's plans will be fulfilled when we cannot see their fulfillment. Joseph's faith in the transformative power of dreams challenges us to hold onto hope, even when things appear bleak. Like him, we too can find our way by moonlight and trust that the dawn will come.

Journey from Darkness to Understanding

Though dreaming is a normal human experience, understanding its meaning is an entirely different matter. The story of Joseph's experiences with the chief cupbearer and the chief baker illustrates this point. While imprisoned with Joseph, both men had dreams that deeply troubled them Their distress was clearly visible and seeing their sorrow, Joseph asked, "Why do you look so sad today?" (Gen 40:7). Their response revealed a problem: "We both had dreams," they said, "but there is no one to interpret them" (Gen 40:8).

They were experiencing a common problem: the frustration of encountering something meaningful but lacking the ability to comprehend it. For the cupbearer and baker, the absence of interpretation rendered their dreams meaningless, leaving them confused and in despair. The truth is that we are unable to understand divine revelation without God's intervention.

Their story reminds us that we live in a world overshadowed by an internal darkness that prevents us from understanding spiritual matters. Without God in our lives, we are like the "walking dead," physically alive but spiritually lifeless. John captures this tragedy when he tells us in his Gospel that though "The light shines in the darkness,... the darkness has not understood it. " (Jn 1:5).

This blindness is our greatest tragedy. Even when the brightest light—Jesus Christ—shines upon the world, we struggle to recognize it. Sin and ignorance obscure our spiritual vision, as we are unable to grasp the meaning of God's revelation. This predicament is poignantly described in Revelation 5:2, where the angels cry out, "Who is worthy to break the seals and open the scroll?" The scroll, symbolizing

God's truth and revelation, lies before us, yet without divine intervention, it remains sealed, inaccessible, and incomprehensible.

Amid this darkness, Joseph emerges with spiritual sight. Despite his own suffering and imprisonment, his faithful relationship with God gave him clarity and understanding and enabled him to perceive and interpret the things of God. Unlike those around him, the despair or circumstances did not blind him. When the cupbearer and baker lamented their inability to understand their dreams, Joseph responded with confidence, "Do not interpretations belong to God? Tell me your dreams" (Gen 40:8). Joseph's confidence stemmed from his reliance on God. He recognized that dreams and their interpretations were part of God's sovereign communication. His faith allowed him to serve as a vessel through which God revealed His truths, making Joseph a beacon of light in the darkness of the prison.

Joseph's story underscores the vital role of divine revelation in overcoming the darkness of human ignorance. Dreams, like God's Word, require divine interpretation to be understood. Without God's revelation, we remain lost, unable to discern the meaning of the signs and truths placed before us. The plight of the cupbearer and baker reflects our collective need for a mediator—someone who can bridge the gap between God's revelation and our understanding. In Joseph's time, he filled this role, interpreting the dreams that perplexed his fellow prisoners. For us, this role is fulfilled perfectly in Jesus Christ. As the Light of the World, Jesus illuminates the darkness and opens the "scroll" of God's truth, enabling us to see, understand, and respond.

The Double-Edged Sword

Joseph's interpretation of the dreams of Pharaoh's servants provides insight into the dual nature of God's dealings with us. The cupbearer's dream foretold restoration to his former position in Pharaoh's palace, while the baker's dream foretold his demise. Two dreams, two contrasting outcomes. This narrative highlights that God's sovereignty operates as a double-edged sword, bringing both blessing and judgment. For God is not only a God of blessing but also of justice. His double-edged sword wields both with equal precision.

At Golgotha, where Jesus was crucified between two criminals. One mocked him, choosing to remain hardened in his sin. The other, however, repented and acknowledged the justice of his punishment, declaring, "We indeed are suffering justly, for we are receiving what we deserve for our deeds' (Lk 23:40-41). The repentant thief was promised paradise, while the other met his end without hope. For God's justice is not arbitrary but responsive to the condition of the heart.

God's judgment is based on a fundamental distinction: those who "know" Him and those who do not. However, this form of "knowing" extends beyond intellectual recognition, encompassing a relational understanding that involves acknowledging one's own sinfulness and recognizing the necessity of God as our Savior. Joseph's interpretation of the dreams illustrates that the cupbearer's restoration and the baker's condemnation were not random; they were divinely appointed outcomes that corresponded to God's purposes.

Similarly, God's purpose for us is revealed as we respond to divine revelation.

Joseph's interpretation of the dreams was remarkably accurate. He delivered God's message exactly as it was revealed, without embellishment or adjustment. There was no "surplus of meaning" or attempt to alter the message to suit his audience. He was a faithful messenger of what God had shown him. Such integrity is crucial because God's truth is not ours to manipulate. It must be proclaimed as it is, regardless of the reactions it receives. Joseph's unwavering commitment to truth demonstrated the courage and faith required to handle God's Word faithfully.

Despite his service to others, Joseph's personal hopes remained unfulfilled. He asked the cupbearer to remember him and speak to Pharaoh on his behalf, pleading his innocence: "I was forcibly carried off from the land of the Hebrews, and even here I have done nothing to deserve being put in a dungeon" (Gen 40:15). Yet, the chief cupbearer forgot him and left Joseph to languish in prison for two more years. This delay is a poignant reminder of the sovereignty of God's timing. While the cupbearer's forgetfulness might seem like an injustice, it was ultimately part of God's plan. Joseph's time in prison prepared him for the role he would later play in Pharaoh's court and the survival of his people.

Chapter 5:
Joseph's Ascension

Faith has its dues. Surely, there is a time for everything—a time to mourn and a time to dance (Eccl. 3:1, 4). When the appointed time arrives, God bestows upon His people "a crown of beauty instead of ashes, the oil of joy instead of mourning, and a garment of praise instead of a spirit of despair" (Isa. 61:3). After faith has endured its season of suffering, its way is paved for glory. Joseph's story exemplifies that the glory of his faith emerged after enduring long and dark hours of tribulation.

His rise to prominence didn't begin with his own dream, but with one belonging to Pharaoh. The king of Egypt had two dreams pointing to the same event, which no one in his court or throughout the land could interpret. This inability underscored the deeper spiritual darkness that pervaded this powerful nation.

Pharaoh's urgent search for the interpretation of his dreams triggered the memory in the chief cupbearer, who suddenly remembered the young Hebrew man he had encountered in prison. Regret filled his heart as he confessed, "Today I am reminded of my shortcomings" (Gen 41:9). He recounted to Pharaoh how Joseph had accurately interpreted both his own dream and that of the chief baker. The precision of Joseph's interpretations left no doubt about his ability.

The cupbearer's standing with Pharaoh gave his words weight and prompted the king to act. He immediately sent for Joseph; he had him brought from the dungeon" (Gen 41:14). After he shaved and changed his clothes, he transformed himself from a prisoner into someone fit to stand before the king.

When Joseph finally stood before Pharaoh, the king addressed him with urgency: "I had a dream, and no one can interpret it. But I have heard it said of you that when you hear a dream, you can interpret it" (Gen 41:15). Joseph's response was a testament to his humility and faith. "I cannot do it," he declared, but then affirmed the source of his confidence, "God will give Pharaoh the answer he desires" (Gen 41:16). Joseph understood his role not as the source of divine insight but as a vessel through whom God's revelation could flow. Such humility and transparency embody the godly character that every follower of Christ should strive to cultivate.

Interpreting Pharaoh's two dreams was easy for Joseph. Though they were separate, they conveyed the same message. Through Pharaoh's dreams, God revealed what was to come, and despite their pagan ways, God's mercy was extended to them while the message remained veiled until Joseph was summoned. As Joseph explained, Egypt would experience "seven years of abundance followed by seven years of famine" (Gen 41:29-30). He emphasized that the repetition of the dream signified the certainty of its fulfillment: "The reason the dream was given to Pharaoh in two forms is that the matter has been firmly decided by God, and God will do it soon" (Gen 41:32).

Joseph understood these dreams on a personal level, for he had received two similar dreams in his youth. His divinely ordained dreams foretold his rise to prominence and the subservience of his brothers. Just as Pharaoh's dreams foretold the destiny of a nation, Joseph's dreams signified his role in preserving his family and people. But, in his younger years, he could not have known how swiftly God would set His plan into motion. From the moment Joseph's journey began, God was working to bring His promises to fruition.

Theology of Nature

Joseph's interpretation was rooted in his understanding that abundance and famine were not mere natural phenomena but acts of God. This raises the question of whether God causes such good or bad events, or are they simply natural processes that occur without divine involvement?

From a modern, materialist perspective, it's easy to dismiss these as predictable occurrences devoid of spiritual significance. This view separates the material from the divine, often regarding belief in God or spiritual influence as irrelevant in today's scientific age. Philosopher John Caputo captured this modern tension with his sharp observation: "Nowadays everyone wants to be a materialist, even the theologians, while the materialists want to look like they lead a spiritual life." His comment reveals the growing complexity of reconciling the material and spiritual dimensions in contemporary thought.

God and matter are not oppositional but work together. God's actions do not negate natural laws; rather, they operate within and alongside God, guiding creation's processes without overriding them. The world exists as a partnership between God, nature, and humanity. While the precise interplay of these forces remains mysterious, one truth emerges: God permits both freedom and order, for God allows the world to move purposefully while remaining faithful to its inherent design.

Joseph's understanding reflects this harmony. He discerned that the seven years of abundance and seven years of famine were not accidents of nature but divine orchestration. For him, there is an inherent duality of good and bad in the created order. This universal truth is recognized beyond Christian theology. Buddhists, for example, acknowledge this tension and seek to overcome it through self-discipline and self-emptying. A spiritually attuned person, like Joseph, sees that having good and bad elements is a fundamental feature of life.

Why, then, does God allow the "bad" to persist? This question invites reflection on the nature of existence. The parable of the weeds in Matthew 13:27–29 illustrates that if the negative aspects of the world were eradicated, the fabric of creation itself might unravel. When the servants offer to uproot the weeds from the field, the owner cautions against it, lest they destroy the wheat as well. The good and bad are intertwined, and their separation must await the right time and method. In the interim, God often addresses the presence of evil by revealing glimpses of the future.

Divine revelation guides through the darkness, as it offers hope and direction. Without such insight, we remain trapped in the limitations of the present—ignorant, self-centered, and consumed by material concerns. This disconnection from the future blinds us to its divine significance. Although the present moment is important, it is intrinsically tied to the future. The present lays the foundation for what is to come, and the future calls us toward the ultimate purpose of God—salvation.

Yet, the future is not easily accessible to all. Human blindness due to ignorance, pride, or distraction renders many incapable of perceiving divine revelation that encompasses it. So mediators, like Joseph, become essential. He acted as a spiritual conduit between God and Pharaoh, unveiling the divine purpose embedded in Pharaoh's dreams. His role exemplifies the need for a spiritual "ladder" connecting heaven and the divine will with earth and human understanding.

Joseph the Great Manager

Joseph's rise to power was marked by a combination of divine wisdom, human diligence, and the unfolding of a remarkable destiny. He not only interpreted Pharaoh's dreams with precision, but also offered inspired, practical counsel. He strategically advised Pharaoh to appoint a trustworthy individual to oversee the collection of one-fifth of the harvest during the years of abundance and store it for the years of famine (Gen 41:33–36). The wisdom of this sound proposal was evident to Pharaoh and all his officials, for as the Scripture records, "The plan seemed good to Pharaoh and to all his officials" (Gen 41:37).

His ability to discern and act wisely was not merely a product of natural intelligence or life experience, but a reflection of the vital truth that wisdom comes from God (Jas 3:17). His years of diligence, integrity, and faithfulness had prepared him for this critical moment, but Joseph never allowed pride to overshadow the divine source of his insight. Pharaoh himself recognized this, declaring, "Since God has made all this known to you, there is no one so discerning and wise as you. You shall be in charge of my palace, and all my people are to submit to your orders. Only with respect to the throne will I be greater than you" (Gen 41:39–40).

The ascent to his position of authority was characterized by a progressive accumulation of trust and responsibility. First, Potiphar entrusted him with the management of his household. Then, the prison warden recognized his reliability and put him in charge of all the prisoners. Finally, Pharaoh placed Joseph in charge of the entire nation's resources. This progression echoes a biblical principle: "Whoever can be trusted with very little can also be trusted with much" (Luke 16:10). Joseph's faithfulness in managing smaller tasks prepared him for the monumental responsibility of overseeing Egypt's food supply and, ultimately, preserving the lives of countless people. In God's providence, Joseph's stewardship extended beyond Egypt to encompass the salvation of the known world.

Pharaoh's actions memorialized Joseph's elevation to power. He gave Joseph his signet ring, clothed him in fine linen, adorned him with a gold chain, and paraded him in the second chariot, with cries of "Bow the knee!" proclaiming his authority over the land (Gen 41:42–43). Joseph, the man once despised and sold as a slave, was now the second most powerful figure in the world. His meteoric rise was nothing short of miraculous, a testament to the sovereignty of God in raising the lowly and fulfilling His promises. Who could have imagined such a transformation—a slave boy becoming the great manager of Egypt?

In this new role, Joseph's ornate robe, once stripped from him in betrayal, was symbolically replaced with royally adorned garments of fine linen. Though not a king, Joseph's authority was nearly equal to Pharaoh's, and everyone was required to bow before him. The Pharaoh decreed this a law, and defiance would result in severe consequences. The one who once dreamed of people bowing to him now saw that dream fulfilled far beyond what he could have imagined.

Joseph was 30 years old when he ascended to power. His years of hardship, betrayal, and imprisonment were not wasted, but had shaped his character and prepared him for the immense task ahead. Reflecting on his transformation, Joseph named his first son Manasseh, meaning, "God has made me forget all my trouble and all my father's household" (Gen 41:51). His second son, Ephraim, was named to signify, "God has made me fruitful in the land of my suffering" (Gen 41:52). These names encapsulate Joseph's profound understanding of God's sovereignty—He had turned pain into purpose, suffering into abundance, and loss into restoration.

Rain and Sunshine

Joseph's testimony resonates with the lyrics of the gospel song, "Give Them All to Jesus."

He never said you only see sunshine,
He never said there would be no rain.
He only promised a heart full of singing,
For the very thing that once brought pain.

The first thirty years of Joseph's narrative were shaped by adversity and sorrow. He endured the disdain of his brothers, who, blinded by ignorance and jealousy, betrayed and sold him into slavery. He was stripped of his home and freedom, falsely accused of a crime he did not commit, and thrown into prison, to languish for years in the shadows, forgotten by those he had helped. Yet, in the midst of this darkness, Joseph clung to his faith in God. His unyielding reliance on God's promises enabled him to persevere through each trial.

Joseph's journey reveals the truth that life under God's care does not guarantee constant sunshine or the absence of storms. Despite being chosen and blessed, Joseph faced hardship and injustice. However, these became the soil in which his faith took root and grew. Each challenge refined his character and deepened his dependence on God. The pain that once defined his life ultimately became the prelude to his triumph, as God's purpose unfolded beyond human comprehension.

When the light of God's glory finally shone on him, Joseph could look back and see the divine hand at work. He understood that the struggles he endured were not random but purposeful and moments of pain and despair became the source for his testimony and his song of praise. Joseph could sing with a heart full of gratitude for the trials that had refined him.

Wastefulness

As Joseph predicted, Egypt was blessed with seven years of abundance "so he gathered up all the food of the seven years …, and… "laid up in every city the food of the fields which surrounded them." Joseph gathered a lot of grain, like the sand of the sea, until he stopped counting, for it was immeasurable" (Gen 41:48–49).

God poured blessings on Egypt, filling the land with an abundance. Yet, as the story of the prodigal son shows us, God's provision often brings out our tendency to waste what we receive. That son, recklessly squandered his father's wealth, reducing himself to destitution in a foreign land. In the end, he was left with nothing, abandoned in a pig pen, and eating scraps meant for animals to survive a famine. His story illustrates how quickly we can misuse the blessings of wealth, time, or talent. Instead of gratefully and responsibly stewarding these gifts, we often take them for granted and squander them, failing to use them for God's glory or the benefit of our community.

Joseph's story carries a similar caution. Though Egypt experienced seven years of plenty, as the famine became severe in the land of Egypt, the surrounding lands, "many had failed to prepare. Having enjoyed abundance, but now having exhausted their resources and facing desperate hunger, all countries came to Joseph to buy grain for relief. (Gen 41:56–57)

Chapter 6:
Joseph's Brothers in Egypt

Joseph's brothers were no better off than the rest of the people. The famine had struck hard, and they were left with no grain. Hearing that Egypt still had supplies, Jacob told his sons, "I have heard that there is grain in Egypt; go down there and buy some for us, so that we may live and not die" (Gen 42:2). So Joseph's older brothers set off to secure the food they desperately needed. However, the youngest brother, Benjamin, stayed behind with their father. Jacob feared for Benjamin's safety, unsure if he could trust his other sons or the journey to a foreign land that seemed fraught with uncertainty.

When the brothers arrived in Egypt, Joseph recognized them immediately, though they were among thousands of travelers. His brothers had not changed much over the years. They were still shepherds, dressed in the familiar attire of rough wool garments, tunics sewn crudely at the sides, and heavy capes draped over their shoulders. They appeared unmistakably as Hebrew nomads, much as Joseph remembered them.

They remained shepherds in their wool tunics and heavy capes, just as Joseph remembered them. But Joseph had changed. The young lad had become a man of influence and power, fully integrated into Egyptian society. Gone were the days of simple tunics; now Joseph wore robes of fine, silky fabric, adorned with gold, and a gold chain hung from his neck. He no longer resembled the naive youth who had been sold into slavery. Joseph was an aristocrat, a man of authority, a father of two sons.

The contrast between him and his brothers was striking—while they remained the same, Joseph had completely changed.

It's no surprise then, "Joseph, while recognizing his brothers, but they did not recognize him" (Gen 42:8).

Despite the intense emotions that stirred within him, Joseph controlled his response. He had two possible paths before him. He could exact revenge by having his brothers thrown into prison, to experience the suffering he had endured. Or he could reveal his identity, invite them into his home, and forgive them for the wrongs they had done to him.

Yet Joseph did not immediately choose either option. Instead, he tested them to see if they had changed and determine whether they were the same men filled with hatred, jealousy, and resentment—who had sold him into slavery. Caught between his past pain and the hope for reconciliation, he waited for the right moment to reveal himself. But the tension in his heart must have been stifling.

Joseph's Play

Joseph looked at his brothers and said sternly, "You are spies! You have come to see the nakedness of the land" (Gen 42:9). This was a serious accusation. In ancient times, being accused of espionage could lead to a swift and brutal death. If Joseph's brothers were found to be spies, they would likely face a painful and humiliating execution. With this accusation, their lives hung in the balance, vulnerable to Joseph's judgment. In that moment, the brothers' fate seemed like a candle flame flickering in the wind, ready to be extinguished at any moment.

But Joseph's actions were not motivated by a desire for revenge or punishment. He was "playing" with them, engaging in a test, much like God had once tested Abraham's faith. God deeply loved Abraham, and after granting him a miracle baby, Isaac, when Abraham was 100 years old, God asked Abraham to sacrifice his beloved son as a test of faith. Abraham had waited so long for Isaac and loved him dearly—perhaps more than anything else. Yet, when God called, Abraham obeyed without question. He took his son to the mountain to fulfill the command, trusting that God had a plan, even if he did not understand it fully.

When Isaac, noticed that the lamb for the sacrifice was missing, asked, "The fire and wood are here, but where is the lamb for the burnt offering?" (Gen 22:7), Abraham responded in faith, saying, "God himself will provide the lamb for the burnt offering, my son" (Gen 22:8). Abraham's words were true. Though he did not know it yet, God had already provided the sacrifice. Isaac was not the true "lamb"—God would supply a ram to be offered in Isaac's stead. With his faith tested, he saw God's provision, and the ram was sacrificed in place of his son (Gen 22:13).

Through this test, God "played" with Abraham—not to cause harm or to mock him, but to reveal and strengthen Abraham's faith. By asking Abraham to sacrifice Isaac, God exposed the depth of his devotion. Abraham's faith was not rooted in his love for Isaac, but in his unwavering trust that God's will was best. This pivotal moment showed Abraham's complete willingness to put God first, even above his most precious earthly possession. Abraham named the place "The Lord Will Provide" (Gen 22:14), a testimony to God's faithfulness and provision.

God's intention was not to test Abraham's faith for His own sake, but to make Abraham's trust visible to all nations to see the greatness of his faith. God wanted to show that Abraham's devotion to Him surpassed everything else, even his cherished son. This deeply agonizing test that had Abraham spending three days walking to the mountain with his son, knowing what was to come, was a powerful and glorious demonstration of Abraham's obedience. The saying "no pain, no gain" captures the essence of Abraham's journey, for through his suffering, his faith was proven and strengthened.

A similar "play" unfolded with Joseph and his brothers. Joseph's intentions were not to harm them, which he could have easily done without the theatrics of this elaborate test. Like God with Abraham, Joseph was testing the hearts of his brothers and allowing them to redeem themselves, reclaim their lost honor, and restore what had been broken by their betrayal. Joseph was offering them a second chance to make things right and show that they had changed since they sold him into slavery.

But Joseph was also inviting them to share in the glory that had been promised to him through his dreams as a young boy. These dreams, which had sparked their jealousy when he once shared them with them, were becoming a reality. This test allowed them to prove whether they had grown in character and were worthy of sharing in the honor he had gained.

A Win-Win Situation

Joseph knew that his brothers were not easily fooled. They had been cunning and resourceful in the past, so he had to be strategic and careful. His plan had to be executed with precision—otherwise, they would see through his ruse before he could uncover the true condition of their hearts. He hoped for some indication of change in them. While their outward appearances may not have changed much, Joseph hoped their hearts had softened. Just as he had matured during his years in Egypt, perhaps they too had grown. With maturity comes reflection, and with reflection comes the realization of past wrongdoings and the remorse that follows.

Joseph kept his brothers in prison for three days. The confinement served to intensify their anxiety and make them feel the weight of the accusation, heightening the tension of the moment. This provided time for Joseph to reflect, while he gave his brothers a taste of the suffering he had endured. Of course, three days could not begin to make up for the years of hardship, affliction, and isolation he had faced in a foreign land. But it let them feel some measure of what he had experienced. These three days of "walking in darkness" were necessary for them to see the light of truth and transformation.

On the third day, Joseph spoke to them: "Let one of your brothers stay here in prison, while the rest of you go and take grain back for your starving households. But you must bring your youngest brother to me, so that your words may be verified and that you may not die" (Gen 42:19-20). The brothers explained that their youngest brother, Benjamin, was with their father. Though they told Joseph the truth, Joseph would not simply take their word. He insisted on verifying their claim. So, Simeon was left behind, and the other brothers returned home, their hearts filled with fear and uncertainty about what awaited them.

Adding to their confusion, Joseph had returned the money they paid for the grain, putting silver back in their sacks. But why? Joseph knew firsthand from his own painful experience what it was like to be sold into slavery for a handful of silver. He understood how greed could blind someone to the value of a human life. By returning the silver, Joseph was testing whether his brothers had truly changed, for if they were still driven by greed, they could simply leave Simeon behind and escape with both the grain and the silver. There would be no consequences for them—they would gain everything and lose nothing. It would be a "win-win" situation for them if they didn't care about the fate of their brother.

On the other hand, if they returned to Joseph, it would be a "lose-lose" situation. They would have to explain why they had not paid for the grain, which would be a difficult conversation, especially when they had kept the silver for themselves. Moreover, they would have to bring Benjamin—a seemingly impossible task. Their father, Jacob, would never willingly let his beloved son go, after everything he had suffered.

The brothers were in a moral bind: were they willing to make a sacrifice, to risk everything for the sake of their brother Simeon and the truth. The dilemma gave them a chance to demonstrate whether they had changed or if they were still the same men who had sold Joseph into slavery years ago.

A Change for Good

Once they reached home, the brothers faced a critical decision that tested their character and commitment to one another. They had to risk everything, including their lives, to return to Joseph, who had set a trap for them. The grain had run out, and their only option was to go back to Egypt. But, once more, Jacob was hesitant to part with his youngest son, Benjamin.

At that moment, Judah stepped forward with a selfless declaration. "Send the boy along with me, and we will go at once, so that we and you and our children may live and not die. I myself will guarantee his safety; you can hold me personally responsible for him. If I do not bring him back to you and set him here before you, I will bear the blame before you all my life" (Gen 43:8-9).

Judah's words were remarkable. Here was a man who had been part of the scheme to sell Joseph into slavery, driven by jealousy and personal gain. But Judah was transformed, and his willingness to put his own life on the line for Benjamin revealed a profound change in his heart. The selfish ambition, power struggles, and envy that had once plagued their family. These were replaced by a willingness to take responsibility for the well-being of others, particularly his family. What had happened to bring about such a change?

The years of regret and shame over their past actions of selling Joseph into slavery—had weighed heavily on them. Judah was no longer the man who had let envy and rivalry dictate his actions. Now, he was willing to bear the consequences of his decisions, even if it meant sacrificing his own future.

Jacob was deeply moved by the sincerity of Judah's plea. The firmness in Judah's voice, his commitment to Benjamin's safety, spoke volumes. Judah meant what he said, and it was evident that he was ready to do whatever it took to right their wrongs. Jacob could not ignore the resolve in his son's words. So, he responded, "Take your brother also and go back to the man at once. And may God Almighty grant you mercy before the man so that he will let your other brother and Benjamin come back with you. As for me, if I am bereaved, I am bereaved" (Gen 43:13-14).

This was a pivotal moment in Jacob's own journey. His words, "If I am bereaved, I am bereaved," echo a sentiment of profound surrender. Like Esther's declaration "If I perish, I perish" (Esth 4:16), it speaks of a complete submission to God's will, regardless of the outcome. In saying this, Jacob was surrendering to the reality that, ultimately, he was not in control. He had done everything he could to protect Benjamin, but now he had to trust God to guide and protect his sons.

Jacob's letting go of his fear and control was a moment of spiritual growth. He was placing his trust in God's hands, acknowledging that only God could bring about a resolution, even if it meant the possibility of further loss. Just as Abraham had entrusted Isaac to God, Jacob now had to place Benjamin into God's care, knowing that, like his grandfather, he was risking the pain of "bereavement" once more. But in doing so, he was acknowledging God's sovereignty over his life and the lives of his children. Jacob, like Abraham, had come to a place of deep faith and surrender, where he was able to say, "Not my will, but Yours be done."

A Second Coming

Joseph's brothers returned to Egypt and were warmly received by Joseph. They came bearing gifts, twice the amount of silver, and Benjamin, as Joseph requested (Gen 43:15). Their gesture satisfied Joseph's demands, and he prepared a feast for them. Concerned about the silver previously found in their sacks, they explained that they had not knowingly taken the silver and were confused about how it had ended up in their sacks. Joseph reassured them, saying, "It's all right. Don't be afraid. Your God, the God of your father, has given you treasure in your sacks; I received your silver" (Gen 43:23).

In truth, Joseph, who had ordered his servants to return the silver to their sacks. However, Joseph's words ring with a deeper truth. The ultimate source of the blessing was not Joseph's alone, but God Himself. It was God who made this provision possible, and Joseph, as God's instrument, rightly affirmed this divine truth. So, his reassurance was a diplomatic gesture as well as a reminder that God's hand was at work in their lives.

The brothers were comforted by Joseph's words, and the tension to lifted, signaling that Joseph's dramatic testing of them might be nearing its end. However, the play was not yet fully over. There were still layers to be uncovered, for Joseph knew that his brothers' transformation was far from complete.

As they feasted, Joseph's emotions began to stir. It was a surreal experience. This moment, this conversation, was both familiar and intensely different. When Joseph was younger, he had always felt like an outsider in the family, relegated to the margins, unable to fully engage in the conversations with his older brothers. He had often waited for his turn to speak, but by the time it came, his brothers would have already dispersed to tend to the sheep, leaving him behind. His voice was rarely heard, and when it was, it was easily dismissed.

But a completely shifted dynamic, he was no longer on the outside. He was at the center of the conversation, the one who initiated it and steered it. His brothers, who once sought to silence him, now sat before him, listening intently. This shift in power and authority was bittersweet for Joseph. Though he had risen to a position of great influence, the emotional weight of this reunion was overwhelming. He was no longer the boy who had dreamed of greatness only to be betrayed and abandoned by his brothers. He was the man who had endured unimaginable hardships, and yet, he was still deeply connected to his brothers.

As Joseph looked around the table at the faces of his brothers—his blood relatives who had caused him so much pain—he was flooded with mixed emotions. There was relief, yes, but also a profound sadness. He had waited so long for this moment, but now that it had arrived, he realized that it wasn't just a moment of victory over his brothers—it was a reminder of the brokenness that had once existed between them.

As the conversation flowed, Joseph was moved by the depth of his feelings. The years of pain, separation, and longing had culminated in this one moment, and though he was now in a position of power, he was still that younger brother who longed for reconciliation, healing, and restoration.

This was not just a meal; it was a turning point in their relationship. And as Joseph watched the interaction unfold, he knew that the journey of forgiveness and redemption was still ongoing. The path forward would require more than just words;

it would demand genuine repentance, humility, and a willingness to restore what had been broken.

The Injustice of the Seats

For the second time, Joseph was overwhelmed by his emotions. The deep feelings of reconciliation, regret, and joy threatened to undo his intricate plan. Had he allowed himself to be swept away by emotion, the carefully constructed "play" would have been ruined. So, once again, Joseph retreated to a private place to weep in solitude. As he composed himself, he knew his role was not yet complete. The show would have to go on. So after washing his face and regaining composure, Joseph returned to his brothers with a calm demeanor and, controlling his emotions, instructed, "Serve the food" (Gen 43:31).

As the meal began, something unusual caught the attention of Joseph's brothers. They were seated in a specific order—arranged according to their ages, from the firstborn to the youngest (Gen 43:33). They looked at each other in astonishment. How could Joseph, whom they thought knew nothing of their family dynamics, have arranged them this way? But what amazed them was the way Benjamin's portion stood out. Joseph had ordered that Benjamin's portion be five times as much as everyone else's (Gen 43:34). This extravagant display of favoritism was no accident, but was part of Joseph's larger plan. It was a carefully orchestrated effort to provoke a reaction from his brothers, to see if they had truly changed. This entire scene was full of subtle clues—hints to reveal Joseph's true identity. But his brothers remained clueless and had no idea who Joseph really was. And they never realized they were being tested.

As "Egyptians could not eat with Hebrews, for that is detestable to Egyptians, " Joseph and his brothers ate together, but the Egyptians had their separate tables. (Gen 43:32). The social and cultural dynamics surrounding this meal speak to a deeper truth about human nature. The political and social structures of society have always been inherently divisive. People are territorial by nature; we want to separate ourselves from those we deem "other," from the "lowly," to align with the "elite."

This tendency can be explained through an evolutionary lens, in which the survival of the fittest compels the strongest to dominate and cast aside the weaker. Both in ancient times and today, society favors the elites. Even with modern social welfare programs and advances in human rights, the uncomfortable truth is that power structures benefit those at the top.

However, every human being is created in the image of God. So we must respect others as we attempt to build a society that is not divided along status or power lines. Such elitism runs counter to the harmonious community that God intended for His creation. As Christians, we must transcend these boundaries to challenge the structures that perpetuate inequality and division.

The prophet Isaiah paints a utopian vision of what such unity could look like. In Isaiah 11:6-9, we read of a time when the world will reflect the harmony and peace that God desires for all His children. This future, where peace reigns and all are reconciled, is a reality we are called to work toward.

Our inability to cross boundaries of division and create a society rooted in love and unity cost God the life of His only Son, Jesus Christ. He came to bridge the divides that have existed throughout human history. His sacrifice on the cross was the ultimate act of reconciliation to restore what had been severed by sin. Through His death and resurrection, Jesus made it possible for us to break down the spirit of elitism.

Yet, the struggle to overcome old habits and prejudices is ongoing. The tendency toward division and exclusion is ingrained in human nature, so the Holy Spirit must help us exercise Christ-like virtues. We must allow the Holy Spirit to work within us, transforming our hearts and minds so that we can embody the love, humility, and grace that Christ demonstrated.

Our prayers echo the longing for this transformation: "Come, Holy Ghost, fill the hearts and minds of Thy faithful servants and enkindle in them the fire of Thy Divine love. Send forth Thy Spirit, and they shall be created, and Thou shalt renew the face of the earth." In this prayer, we invite the Holy Spirit to renew the entire world, healing the divisions that separate us and restoring the unity that God intended.

Are We Righteous?

As morning broke, Joseph's brothers were sent on their way, but Joseph had one last test for them, and his elaborate plan had reached its climax. He instructed his steward, "Fill the men's sacks with as much food as they can carry, and put each man's silver in the mouth of his sack. Then put my silver cup in the mouth of the youngest one's sack, along with the silver for his grain" (Gen 44:1-2). He had set a snare that his brothers could not escape.

Joseph's instructions to his steward were clear: "Go after those men at once, and when you catch up with them, say to them, 'Why have you repaid good with evil? Isn't this the cup my master drinks from and uses for divination? This is a wicked thing you have done" (Gen 44:4-5). Though we know that Joseph's brothers did not steal the cup and were innocent of the crime, the circumstances Joseph set in motion made them appear guilty. They were about to face a dire crisis.

As the steward caught up with them and accused them of theft, Joseph's brothers were bewildered. They asserted their innocence. "We even brought back… the silver we found inside the mouths of our sacks. So why would we steal silver or gold from your master's house? If any of your servants is found to have it, he will die; and the rest of us will become my lord's slaves" (Gen 44:8). Their defense seemed righteous, and they were confident to the point of offering their lives as proof of their innocence. Yet, this very confidence in their righteousness would prove to be their undoing.

The truth is that we can never be fully certain of our righteousness. Human nature is messy, and we are not righteous on our own. As the Apostle Paul writes, "None is righteous… no one seeks for God. All have turned aside; together they have become worthless; no one does good, not even one" (Rom 3:10-12). Paul echoes the sentiments of Psalms 14:1-3, reminding us that we all have turned away from God. Our self-assurance in our own righteousness is misplaced and blinds us to the truth of our fallen condition. We, like Joseph's brothers, may not fully recognize our unrighteousness until we are caught in a moment of crisis.

In their certainty, Joseph's brothers, found themselves in a position in which they could not deny their guilt. Joseph warned them, "Whoever is found to have it will become my slave; the rest of you will be free from blame" (Gen 44:10). Convinced of their innocence, his brothers agreed to this condition. They were so sure of their own righteousness that they set the stakes of their defense high, offering their lives as proof of their integrity.

But the moment of reckoning came when the steward searched their belongings, and the missing cup was found in Benjamin's sack, where Joseph had planted it. This was the turning point of the entire drama—Joseph had already sealed the outcome, and his brothers were caught in the snare. They had been played by the circumstances Joseph had created. There was no way around it; the truth had come to light, and they could not defend themselves.

Joseph's brothers were confident, even boastful, of their innocence, but they were blind to the truth of their own hearts. Their easily proclaimed righteousness was exposed as empty when faced with undeniable evidence. They would be forced to confront their flaws and guilt—not just toward Joseph, but toward God. This reveals a truth about human nature and the nature of righteousness.

Like the brothers, we are tempted to overestimate our own righteousness, become self-assured, and point fingers at others, as if we are beyond reproach. However, left to our own devices, we are all far from righteous. True righteousness is not something we can claim, but must be granted through grace. The moment we forget this, we risk being ensnared by our own self-deception. In the face of undeniable evidence, Joseph's brothers would learn the hard truth about their own hearts. They had been played by Joseph, but in reality, they were being played by their own pride and self-righteousness. This harsh lesson was necessary for their transformation.

As intricate as it seemed, Joseph's game was not only designed to expose their guilt but to bring them to repentance and reconciliation. In this process, Joseph's brothers came face to face with their own flaws, and only then could they recognize Joseph for who he truly was. The journey toward righteousness often begins with the painful realization that we are not as righteous as we think we are and that we are in need of a righteous Savior.

The Last Plea

There seemed to be no way out of the situation, and the brothers had lost Benjamin to slavery. In that moment, Judah addressed the matter head-on. He promised his father to return Benjamin safely, and now faced the possibility of their brother being permanently lost to them. So he said to Joseph, "God has uncovered your servants' guilt. We are now my lord's slaves—we ourselves and the one who was found to have the cup" (Gen 44:16). Judah proposed a collective punishment: since one of his brothers had transgressed, then all of them should be treated the same way.

Judah's proposal that all would suffer for the actions of one was a hard choice that echoed the brothers' actions in taking vengeance on the entire city of Shechem, when they because of one man's wrong in raping their sister. What he was suggesting was a return to this harsh, unforgiving cycle. However, having risen above his brothers' past cruelty, Joseph was unwilling to repeat such a cycle. "Far be it from me to do such a thing! Only the man found with the cup will become my slave. The rest of you, go back to your father in peace" (Gen 44:17).

However, Judah's plea was not one of self-preservation or an attempt to protect the brothers as a group. It was an appeal to a sense of justice. If Joseph wanted to see the right thing done, Judah insisted that punishment must only fall on Benjamin, the one who committed the offense, while the others should go free.

The situation had reached a point of no return for Judah and his brothers. It was a matter of life and death. They could not bargain for their freedom. Benjamin was the youngest and most beloved by their father; his loss would devastate their father and show their failure to keep their promise. Judah had to do something extreme that would show Joseph and their father that they were no longer the same men who had betrayed Joseph and abandoned him to slavery.

In a final act of desperation, Judah poured out his heart to Joseph. Speaking truthfully about their father's grief, and how deeply his life was intertwined with Benjamin's., he said, "If I do not bring him back to you, my father will die" (Gen 44:22). In describing their bond, he continued, "His life is closely bound up with the boy's life," and truthfully told Joseph that if he were to return without Benjamin, their father would not survive the heartbreak (Gen 44:31). Then he made a J remarkable offer that signaled his willingness to sacrifice himself for his brother, saying to Joseph, "Let your servant remain here as my lord's slave in place of the boy, and let the boy return with his brothers" (Gen 44:33).

With this, Joseph saw that this was not the same Judah who had once callously sold him into slavery. The heart that had once been hardened by jealousy and deceit was now soft and willing to make the ultimate sacrifice. Judah was not only asking for mercy for Benjamin, but he was demonstrating that he had changed. He was offering his own freedom, his own life, to save his brother and protect their father, and this showed that he and his brothers were no longer the men they once were.

Judah's plea to Joseph was a turning point. In that moment, Judah's plea was not just a cry for Benjamin's life; it was a declaration of the brothers' repentance and genuine concern for one another. Their earlier deceit, betrayal, and cruelty had been replaced with a desire to right their wrongs, to take responsibility, and to sacrifice for the ones they loved. His plea marked the moment when the brothers, once separated by sin and guilt, became a united family, bound together by love.

Judah's offer was the key to Joseph's heart, and it would bring about the reconciliation that had been long-awaited. Joseph's response to Judah's plea changed everything. The layers of deceit, betrayal, and resentment that had separated him from his brothers would soon be peeled away.

The End of the Play Final

Joseph finally revealed his true identity. Ending the dramatic play he had orchestrated to test them. For it had served its purpose—to give them the opportunity for repentance, and allow God's larger plan to unfold. Now, the time for secrets and deception had passed.

Overcome with emotion, Joseph wept for a third time. But this time, his weeping was no quiet release of emotion. Instead, he wept openly, with tears so loud that they were heard by the Egyptians who were outside the room. This was a raw, unrestrained, and powerful display of the deep feelings he had

The emotional scene struck his brothers with terror. For they saw before them a man who, in their minds, had once been their helpless, young brother—now standing as the most powerful man in Egypt, second only to Pharaoh himself. His weeping only intensified their fear, and they had no idea what to expect. Joseph was their enemy whom they had grievously wronged. They felt as vulnerable as Daniel in the lion's den, and death seemed imminent.

To their astonishment, however, Joseph calmed them. His words were not those of a vengeful enemy, but of a brother who had found a way to forgive. And he reassured them that he bore no grudge. Then Joseph briefly recounted the events that had brought him to his position and emphasized that it was not his brothers who had sent him to Egypt, but God Himself. As Joseph put it, "You meant evil against me, but God meant it for good, to bring it about that many people should be kept alive, as they are today" (Gen 50:20).

At that moment, the brothers saw that God's sovereign plan had been at work all along, even in their betrayal. What could have been a devastating moment of certain death had become a scene and an occasion for reconciliation. A few minutes earlier, they had feared for their lives, but now they stood on the threshold of joy. They realized that the brother they sold into slavery was not only alive but elevated to a position of power and influence. Benjamin, the youngest, who had been the object of Joseph's earlier test, embraced him, recognizing that the Egyptian governor standing before him was not his enemy, but his beloved brother, Joseph.

Their fear turned into amazement, which later gave way to joyful celebration. Their "lost" brother was not only forgiving them but embracing them with open arms. Joseph's heart overflowed with grace as he welcomed them into his presence and showered them with extravagant hospitality. As his tears flowed freely, he kissed each of them, signaling the end to the long-held animosity—a moment made possible by God's grace. They were no longer haunted by the sins of their past but were embraced by the love and forgiveness that only God could provide.

Once hardened by guilt and fear, Joseph's brothers now met with grace and forgiveness. They no longer stood as strangers at odds with him but were reconciled, freed from the weight of their past wrongs, and were no longer family once again. As the tension unwound, they spoke openly with words marked by the tenderness of the moment.

Joseph's tears were not only for his own release and joy, but for the fulfillment of God's plan in their lives. What had been meant for harm had been turned into a moment of healing and restoration for a family torn apart by struggle. That healing brought a new beginning built on forgiveness, grace, and God's sovereignty. The years of struggle seem only a distant dream for all of them.

Chapter 7:
The Fruit of Joseph's Faith

This news of the dramatic family reunion reverberated throughout Egypt. When Pharaoh heard about the event, he responded with extraordinary generosity, instructing Joseph to "Tell your brothers,… Load your animals and return to the land of Canaan, and bring your father and your families back to me. I will give you the best of the land of Egypt, and you can enjoy the fat of the land" (Gen 45:17-18). Pharaoh's hospitality exceeded even Joseph's. Surely, God's blessings overflowed through Joseph's faithfulness to reach not only his family but the broader world. God's favor upon Joseph became a vessel for abundant provision for Jacob and his household.

The young boy's dream was not an empty vision; it was the divine promise of God's abundant blessing. Once mocked and misunderstood, that dream became the tool God used to bring salvation and restoration. Not only was Joseph elevated to the highest rank in Egypt, second only to Pharaoh, but God used his leadership to preserve countless lives, including his own family. Joseph's faith became the foundation of a blessing so vast that even his estranged brothers were granted the best land in Egypt. With such abundance, they established a legacy that would grow into the nation of Israel. In this stunning transformation, a family rose from the ashes of betrayal, famine, and despair to the pinnacle of prosperity.

Pharaoh's generosity did not stop there. He commanded Joseph to "take some carts from Egypt for your children and your wives, and get your father and come. Never mind about your belongings, because the best of all Egypt will be yours." (Gen 45:19-20). This command shows the unparalleled favor Jacob's family received. Pharaoh's gifts were displayed in a royal procession: carts laden with new clothes, sacks full of silver, ten donkeys loaded with the finest treasures of Egypt, and ten female donkeys carrying grain, bread, and provisions. And an accompaniment of soldiers to protect them. The caravan was a magnificent sight, drawing the eyes of all who saw it along the way from Egypt back to Canaan. The family was treated as conquering heroes, though their only merit was being related to the man through whom God was working mightily.

When the brother told him, 'Joseph is still alive! In fact, he is the ruler of all Egypt. Jacob was stunned, skeptical, and overwhelmed by the news that Joseph was alive after years of mourning him. Initially, he did not believe them. But when they told him everything Joseph had said to them, and when he saw the carts Joseph had sent to carry him back, the spirit of their father revived, and he said, 'I'm convinced! My son Joseph is still alive. I will go and see him before I die" (Gen 45:26-28). Thus, Jacob's doubt gave way to faith as he realized God's providence at work.

En route to Egypt, Jacob stopped at Beersheba, the southernmost boundary of the Promised Land. Significantly, this place, Beersheba, symbolized a threshold between the land of his ancestors and the unknown future that awaited in Egypt.

This location marked the end of Jacob's journey in the land God had promised to him, Abraham, and Isaac. Aware of the spiritual significance of this departure, Jacob offered sacrifices to God at Beersheba, a site with significant patriarchal history, "where God had spoken to him in a night, 'Jacob! Jacob!' ... Do not be afraid to go down to Egypt, for I will make you into a great nation there. I will go down to Egypt with you, and I will surely bring you back again. And Joseph's own hand will close your eyes.'" (Gen 46:2-4).

Leaving Canaan was not merely a physical relocation for Jacob; it represented a potential spiritual separation from the God of his fathers. Ancient people thought land and deity to be inseparable. Yet God, in His mercy, reassured Jacob that His covenant promises were not bound by geography.

Hearing Faith

God's word guaranteed Jacob that "Israel" would not only survive but flourish as a great nation and eventually return to the land promised to his ancestors. This divine assurance was sweet to Jacob's ears and came at just the right time. In his last recorded encounter with God, Jacob was strengthened by the sweet sound of God's promise. With newfound courage and faith, he pressed on toward Egypt, free of remorse or hesitation.

But why hadn't God spoken to him earlier? Why didn't God tell Jacob that Joseph was alive during those years of pain? Jacob had endured the agony of losing his most beloved son. Yet, while it seemed as though God was silent, God had used Joseph's dreams to foretell that his son would rise to prominence and power. But Jacob had not fully grasped what God was saying. His faith had faltered, and he failed to "hear" the voice of God. Jacob's inability to hear God's promise left him blind to the future God had planned. For when faith stops listening, it stops seeing.

This principle echoes in the New Testament when Jesus chastised His disciples for their "little" faith. "You of little faith, why are you so afraid?" (Matt 8:26). Overwhelmed by the storm, the disciples sat paralyzed, unable to trust in Jesus' power to save them. Their lack of faith threw them into confusion and despair, making them helpless victims of their circumstances. When our faith falters, we, too, find ourselves consumed by fear and uncertainty. These emotions can tear us apart, wounded and prone to blaming God for perceived neglect.

But God has given us faith as a powerful tool to overcome our fears and adversities. It enables us to see beyond the present situation to grasp the extraordinary possibilities of God's power. Our faith is not rooted in our strength but in the God who works through us. For as Paul reminds us, "When I am weak, then I am strong." (2 Cor.12:10). With faith, the impossible becomes possible, and God's power is made manifest.

Jacob eventually regained his faith and began to see how God had been with him all along. Jacob finally understood that God's hand was upon his life and the lives of his sons, the entire time. While his lack of faith had once caused him to lose sight of God's promises, his restored faith enabled him to find his beloved son again.

So Jacob gathered his entire household—all sixty-six members of his family—and set out for Egypt, leaving nothing behind. It was a remarkable exodus from Canaan, a land tied to the covenant promises, to Egypt, a foreign land of opportunity but also potential danger. Jacob's relocation, however, was both a blessing and a foreshadowing of hardship. Though his family prospered initially, many centuries later, his descendants would become slaves in Egypt. The faith-filled leadership seen in Joseph was missing after his death, and the power to break the bondage of slavery was absent until another man of faith, Moses, arose 430 years later (Exod 2:40).

The climax of the story occurred when Joseph went to Goshen to reunite with his father. "As soon as Joseph appeared before him, he threw his arms around his father and wept for a long time." (Gen 46:29). This was the fourth recorded instance of Joseph weeping—a poignant reminder that his story is one of struggle, tears, and triumph. The reunion of father and son was a moment of profound healing and joy. For Jacob, it brought closure to years of grief and sorrow. "Now I am ready to die, since I have seen for myself that you are still alive," Jacob declared (Gen 46:30).

At last, Jacob's fractured family was made whole. The brothers who had once betrayed Joseph now stood together as a united family. Though they were in a foreign land, they were no longer divided by jealousy, deceit, or mistrust. Their physical relocation to Egypt mirrored their spiritual and emotional restoration as a family. What began as a story of pain and brokenness ended with unity, forgiveness, and God's abundant provision.

The Settlement

When Joseph brought his father and brothers before Pharaoh, he carefully selected five out of his twelve brothers for the audience. With this strategic decision, Joseph wanted to ensure that those who stood before the king could present themselves appropriately. Given their background as shepherds—an occupation viewed with disdain by the Egyptians- Joseph probably prepared them in advance on the proper decorum in Pharaoh's presence. When they stood before the king, they spoke with one voice. "We have come to live here for a while, because the famine is severe in Canaan and your servants' flocks have no pasture. So now, please let your servants settle in Goshen" (Gen 47:4).

Though Pharaoh had already granted them permission to reside there, the formal act of presenting their request before him was protocol. Just as Joseph's brothers stood before Pharaoh with reverence and humility, so too should we approach God in prayer. Though we are His children, He is still the King of kings. Our petitions before Him should not be disrespectful or thoughtless; rather, they should be offered with the reverence and honor due to His majesty.

Pharaoh's response was generous: He gave Joseph's father and brothers the best part of the land, told him, " If you know of any among them with special ability, put them in charge of his royal livestock" (Gen 47:5-6). Joseph's brothers became royal managers like Joseph. The new title and position of responsibility and trust elevated their status and ensured their protection. No one in Egypt could mistreat Jacob's family without consequence. They were now under the dual safeguard of Joseph's authority and Pharaoh's royal decree.

The End of Struggle

The season of struggle had ended. Jacob, Joseph, and his brothers had endured many trials. They wrestled with their own hearts, one another, the people around them, the harshness of nature, and even with God. Their lives had been marked by hardship, conflict, and uncertainty.

When Pharaoh met Jacob, he asked him a simple yet profound question: "How old are you?" Jacob's response carried the weight of a lifetime of trials: "The years of my pilgrimage are a hundred and thirty. My years have been few and difficult, and they do not equal the years of the pilgrimage of my fathers" (Gen 47:9).

Though his years were fewer than those of Abraham, who lived to 175, and Isaac, who reached 180, Jacob had walked a difficult path. His words reflected the hardships he had endured—years of deception, exile, family strife, and loss. Yet now, those struggles had come to an end. No longer a wandering shepherd fleeing from enemies or mourning the loss of his beloved son, he could finally settle in peace. The family that had once been scattered and broken was now reunited, living in prosperity under the favor of Egypt's ruler.

But what comes after struggle? For Joseph, it was time to serve those still in distress. As the famine ravaged Egypt and the surrounding nations, he took up the responsibility of sustaining the people. The grain he had stored during the years of abundance became their salvation. Yet the true source of deliverance was not Joseph, but the God who had guided him through his own trials and raised him up for such a time as this. To God be the glory!

Desperate for food, the people of Egypt came to Joseph. They were willing to exchange everything they owned for grain. Their livestock, their land, and even their freedom were surrendered to Pharaoh in exchange for survival. This arrangement strengthened the king's power and stabilized the economy. By requiring the people to give a fifth of their harvest to Pharaoh, Joseph implemented a system that allowed Egypt to prepare for future crises. At the time, it seemed like a fair bargain—no one complained.

However, the expansion of Pharaoh's power had long-term consequences. While the system Joseph established benefited the current ruler, it would one day be exploited by a king who "did not know about Joseph" (Exod 1:8). The very policies that had secured Egypt's prosperity would later contribute to the oppression of Jacob's descendants. The wealth and power of an Egyptian king gave way to the exploitation of the Jewish nation.

Jacob's family had never intended to stay in Egypt permanently. His sons hinted at their desire to return to Canaan when the time was right. After Jacob's death, his final journey was a return home. His funeral was a grand event, unlike anything seen before for a Hebrew shepherd. "All Pharaoh's officials—the dignitaries of his court and all the dignitaries of Egypt—besides all the members of Joseph's household and his brothers and those belonging to his father's household. Chariots and horsemen went up with him. It was a very large company" (Gen 50:8).

Jacob returned to Canaan not as a wandering exile, but as a revered patriarch. His funeral procession, filled with the highest officials of Egypt, resembled the triumphant march of a victorious general. His legacy was undeniable. Though he had once fled Canaan with nothing but his staff, he returned in honor, his name forever established in the history of God's people. Yet even this grand homecoming was nothing compared to the welcome he would receive in eternity. Just as the prodigal son's father clothed him with a robe, ring, and sandals upon his return (Lk 15:22), God welcomed Jacob home with eternal honor.

Joseph, too, eventually passed away (Gen 50:22-26). Before his death, he made his family swear an oath: "God will surely come to your aid, and then you must carry my bones up from this place" (Gen 50:25). It was more than a request—it was a prophecy. Though they lived in prosperity for the time being, their destiny was not in Egypt. They would return to the land of Canaan, just as God had promised.

However, the Israelites soon forgot their purpose. Generations passed, and instead of preparing for their return, they became comfortable in Egypt. When a new Pharaoh arose—one who did not remember Joseph—the people found themselves trapped in a new kind of struggle: slavery. They remained in bondage for centuries until God raised up another dreamer, Moses, to lead them home. The cycle of struggle had not truly ended. But through it all, God was with them.

Epilogue:
The True Color of Faith

Faith is like a dream—it cannot be earned or manufactured. It comes from beyond and reveals mysteries that cannot be grasped by human reason alone. Since it originates from God, faith grants access to the unseen, even to the great Mystery that is God Himself. Though our understanding remains partial, faith allows us to dimly glimpse divine realities. Yet, only the pure in heart can see clearly. Only those with sincerity and devotion can clearly perceive God's vision and grasp the meaning of the dreams He imparts.

We don't acquire faith solely through personal effort. Rather, a transcendent source provides insight into realities beyond human reasoning. As originating from God, it enables us to engage aspects of the unseen, including the divine mystery of God Himself. While human understanding is limited, faith permits awareness of spiritual truths. Clear perception of these realities, however, is reserved for those who demonstrate purity of heart, sincerity, and devotion, as those who can best comprehend God's revelations and interpret inspired dreams.

Surely, not all dreams or visions are divine; only those God reveals serve His purpose. For this reason, dreams and faith are closely connected. Without dreams, spiritual vision fades, and resistance to God's work grows. Still, faith is essential for pursuing and realizing these dreams.

Faith is not an isolated intellect or emotion, but joins mind, soul, and will. Through faith, we make sense of our world. It harmonizes our inner world and helps us understand reality. However, when neglected, faith can weaken or be misplaced as Jacob once neglected once dd. When it loses its power to reconcile, restore, and unite, the mind, soul, and spirit are left in darkness.

Weak, lifeless faith leads to physical, moral, or spiritual decay. Without genuine faith, reason becomes shallow, emotions turn volatile, and the will loses direction, leaving us adrift, unable to stand against life's challenges.

God does not abandon those whose faith is weak. Instead, He restores and breathes new dreams and hopes into weary hearts. Since God cannot lie, His dreams are not wishful thinking, illusions, or fleeting ideals. Every vision He grants reveals what is certain to come to pass. It is grounded in divine truth and the eternal nature of His will.

However, divine dreams require a mediator to bring them to life. For no matter how glorious, a dream must be activated. Someone must receive it, nurture it, and draw out its full potential. But not just anyone can carry such a task. God seeks those with pure hearts and unshakable faith, those who can withstand trials, resist temptation, and endure suffering without losing sight of His promises.

Though Joseph saved Egypt, he could not save the world. Though he provided grain, he could not provide eternal life. God sent someone greater than Joseph—Jesus became that mediator. Though He was exalted, He humbled Himself beyond measure. Without wavering, He stepped into the darkness of human suffering and paid the price with His life. Through His sacrifice, it is possible for us to dream again, faith was restored, and hope became possible.

Now, the responsibility falls to us. Jesus has paved the way, but we must walk in His footsteps. We must be purified to prepare to receive God's visions and make them real. Through faith, we can fulfill God's call to extend the kingdom of God to the ends of the earth.

True faith is not passive belief. Rather, it is an active pursuit. It is the bridge between the seen and the unseen—between the dream and its fulfillment. God is still seeking those who will believe, dream, and stand firm. Will you be among them?

www.ingramcontent.com/pod-product-compliance
Lightning Source LLC
Chambersburg PA
CBHW061035050726
47592CB00004B/1454